GALVESTON'S
JUNETEENTH STORY

GALVESTON'S
JUNETEENTH STORY
AND STILL WE RISE

GALVESTON HISTORICAL FOUNDATION WITH TOMMIE BOUDREAUX,
ALICE GATSON, JAMI DURHAM AND W. DWAYNE JONES

THE
History
PRESS

Published by The History Press
Charleston, SC
www.historypress.com

First published 2024

Manufactured in the United States

ISBN 9781467155274

Library of Congress Control Number: 2023946828

To shining the light that all might see, to telling the real story of our ancestors and to our ancestors, who always knew they would rise.

General Orders No. 3 was issued on June 19, 1865. It announced to the people of Texas that all slaves were free and is the center of one of Galveston's most important historical moments. This day has come to be known as Juneteenth, Freedom Day or Emancipation Day and has been marked by remembrances and celebrations almost every year since. This companion book to the interactive experience *And Still We Rise…Galveston's Juneteenth Story*, exhibited at the 1859 Ashton Villa, introduces the context and consequences of that announcement from 1865 to the present day on a long journey toward "absolute equality."

CONTENTS

FOREWORD

Juneteenth celebrates one of the most important transition points in American history. On June 19, 1865, General Orders No. 3 was issued in Galveston, Texas, marking the practical end of slavery in the state. This was important, because Texas was home to the last major pocket of enslaved individuals in the Confederacy.

Although Juneteenth has now become the basis for a national holiday, many Americans wonder how and why this date emerged as the basis for the oldest continually celebrated commemoration of the end of slavery. To even begin to answer these questions, it is necessary to return to the historic roots of the event itself.

And Still We Rise…Galveston's Juneteenth Story is the first museum exhibit to explore in detail Galveston's unique role in the origin of the Juneteenth story. Galveston ended the Civil War as the last major Confederate port, and Texas ended the war with a population of enslaved individuals that probably numbered at least 250,000. Texas never experienced large Union armies moving through its interior the way other Confederate states had. This meant that when Union soldiers finally landed in Galveston and began enforcing emancipation, their actions brought enormous changes to not only the people directly affected but also the economy and social fabric of Texas.

The discussions of Juneteenth that appear annually in the news media usually associate the celebration with the arrival of General Gordon Granger in Galveston and the issuance of the third of his general orders declaring that slavery was at an end. But the situation was more complex than many celebrants appreciate. One of the most interesting topics explored in the *And Still We Rise* exhibit is the almost contradictory content of the Juneteenth order itself. The four-sentence order began with a bold statement that due to President Abraham Lincoln's Emancipation Proclamation, "All slaves are free." The last two sentences, however, instructed the freed people to stay where they were and to continue working for the people who had enslaved them. If this was freedom, it was of the particularly restrictive variety. Juneteenth has, in some ways, come to symbolize the important contradictions inherent in emancipation at the end of the Civil War.

The second sentence of the Juneteenth order boldly declared that freedom "involves an absolute equality of personal rights and rights of property between masters and slaves." This language—by far the most elegant and meaningful language in the Juneteenth order—was an unfulfilled promise that would soon be challenged by the violence of Reconstruction and its bloody aftermath. *And Still We Rise* chronicles the ways in which emancipation did not lead to "absolute equality" and recalls the stories of people who have struggled ever since to rise from adversity and achieve that bold goal.

Juneteenth provides an annual opportunity for Americans to reflect on how far this country has come from the terrible period when over four million people were enslaved. Almost as soon as the ink on the Juneteenth order was dry, people who had been enslaved began celebrating the events of Juneteenth to recall the challenges and opportunities that were associated with the dramatic end of that evil institution. Their descendants have been celebrating it ever since. At the same time, Juneteenth provides all Americans with an annual opportunity to recommit themselves to the goal of achieving absolute equality for all citizens. Galveston was indeed the origin of Juneteenth, but the ripples from the island's freedom story have now reached the rest of the nation and, increasingly, the world.

Edward T. Cotham Jr.
Civil War historian and author

ACKNOWLEDGEMENTS

With great appreciation, the authors would like to acknowledge the contributions and assistance provided by Allan Smith and Jerry Hewitt of the Gibson Group, New Zealand; military historian Edward Cotham Jr.; Sean McConnell and Kevin Kinney at the Galveston and Texas History Center at Rosenberg Library (Galveston); the Old Central Cultural Center Inc. (Galveston); Kelly Caldwell at the Moody Medical Library at University of Texas Medical Branch (Galveston); the staff of the Houston Public Library's African American Library at the Gregory School; and Lisa Keys at the Kansas State Historical Society. In addition, the authors also appreciate the assistance provided by the Austin History Center, the Texas State Library and Archives Commission (Austin), the Briscoe Center for American History at the University of Texas (Austin), the Library of Congress and the Portal to Texas History/University of North Texas (Denton), as well as Bernard Curtis, Lucious Pope and the families of John Clouser, Courtney Murray and Dr. R.H. Stanton.

Prologue

THE MAKING OF *AND STILL WE RISE…*
GALVESTON'S JUNETEENTH STORY

This exhibit is designed not to take visitors back into the past but to bring the past—living and breathing—into the present. So, it makes much use of authentic historical documents that express and frame the lived experience of African Americans before and after June 19, 1865.

Among the many sources consulted, the Rosenberg Library (Galveston, Texas) and the Library of Congress yielded particularly amazing records of these experiences and none more vivid than *The Slave Narratives*, which record the personal experiences of hundreds of African Americans who were enslaved on Texas plantations and in urban servitude and included over thirty narratives with direct connections to Galveston. While acknowledging the reservations of historians over the methodology that produced *The Slave Narratives*, these personal historical accounts nevertheless go straight to our hearts and souls today, bringing the acknowledgment that Juneteenth is as much an emotional experience as it is a series of facts.

The exhibit brings a deliberately contemporary lens to those historical experiences by allowing us to see them through the eyes of African American families living in Galveston today, some of whom can trace their lineage to the era before the proclamation of General Orders No. 3, during times when enslaved labor built the very building in which the exhibit is housed. And all can relate to the pure joy of that first Juneteenth as described in *Narratives* by Jakob Brank: "Old man Charley so happy he jes' roll on de floor like a hoss and kick he heels."

But our contemporary voices also help us trace the pain of "man's inhumanity to man," as one participant described the horrors of the period of enslavement and its long aftermath. They help us see that the promise of "complete equality" is a promise that remains to be fully achieved; that amid the joy of Juneteenth's celebration of freedom, the pain and struggle continue.

Such an important and complex topic is almost impossible to adequately convey in a short visitor experience. We have tried to offer multiple layers of content so that visitors can find the depth and breadth that works for them, and we make much use of digital interactivity that offers multiple pathways through that content. Interactive timelines trace the headlines of history leading up to and beyond General Orders No. 3 and offer links to experiences in Galveston today. Interactive videos offer visitors curated extracts from many hours of interviews filmed with our contemporary Galveston participants.

It is our hope that this multilayered approach will compel visitors to return time and time again and still find something fresh. The exhibit *And Still We Rise…Galveston's Juneteenth Story* is, like the lived experience of Juneteenth, a work in progress.

Allan Smith, creative producer/co-owner
Gibson Group, New Zealand

1

GALVESTON BEFORE 1865

In 1808, Britain and the United States banned the international trade of enslaved people, but the domestic slave trade continued until the end of the Civil War. The first documented slave in Texas was Estevanico, an African enslaved to a Spanish nobleman who accompanied a Spanish exploration of America and washed ashore on Galveston Island after a storm. Galveston was one of the forty-eight known ports of entry in the United States for enslaved Africans who survived the transatlantic crossing and was a base camp for pirates who plundered slave ships operating outside the ban on transatlantic slave trading. Cuban ships were the main targets, as Cuba was a major depot during the illegal slave trade. A Middle Passage marker at Galveston's Pier 22 commemorates the enslaved Africans who were transported to Galveston during the late eighteenth and early nineteenth centuries, as well as the millions of captive Africans who perished during the transatlantic crossing.

By 1860, Galveston was known as the largest slave market west of New Orleans and the largest city in Texas, shipping 75 percent of the state's cotton, which was produced on plantations where 182,000 enslaved people worked. Around 1,000 of these people were enslaved in Galveston as laborers and servants. Many more enslaved people passed through the city's slave trading houses.

During the nineteenth century, ships from around the world came to Galveston, a major seaport town, to trade goods, auction enslaved people and relay information. Jean Lafitte (1776–1823) was a pirate, privateer and slave trader who patrolled the Gulf of Mexico. He settled in New Orleans

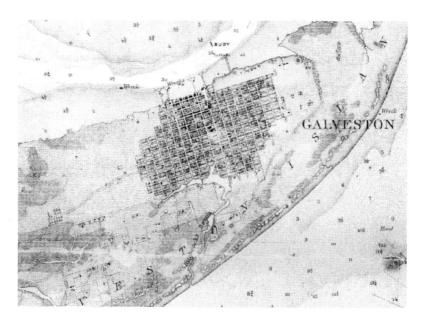

Top: The eastern tip of Galveston Island and the city of Galveston as mapped in 1856. *Courtesy of the Galveston Historical Foundation.*

Bottom: Looking west down the Strand in 1861 from the rooftop of the Hendley building. *Street Files Collection; courtesy of the Rosenberg Library (Galveston, TX).*

Top: The Hendley building (extant) at 20th Street and the Strand as seen from the wharf in 1861. *Street Files Collection; courtesy of the Rosenberg Library (Galveston, TX).*

Bottom: An 1861 view of the city looking south from the Hendley building. *Street Files Collection; courtesy of the Rosenberg Library (Galveston, TX).*

A view of the wharf northeast of the Hendley building in 1861. *Street Files Collection; courtesy of the Rosenberg Library (Galveston, TX).*

with his family around 1780; there, he and his brother profited from the slave trading business for several years. After they were run out of New Orleans in 1817, the Lafitte brothers relocated their business to Galveston, where they continued their slave smuggling business. One of their more famous clients was James Bowie, who bought enslaved people from the Lafitte brothers for one dollar per pound. Bowie was a smuggler and trader from Kentucky who was killed during the Texas Revolution at the historic Battle of the Alamo. Taking advantage of the American laws against the importation of enslaved people from foreign countries, Bowie would report his purchased enslaved people as having been found in the possession of smugglers. He would then collect a fee on the recovered enslaved people, whom he would then rebuy and sell to other buyers at a profit.

Beginning in 1821, when Anglo-Americans from other southern states settled in Texas, bringing enslaved people with them, the numbers of Black people living in the state increased. These settlers held enslaved people as an important source of free labor. For merchants and plantation owners near Galveston, the use of free laborers in cotton fields and toiling in other areas meant profit margins were extremely high. The Strand, the main avenue in the business district, flourished. Over time, the majority of Black people who entered Galveston were enslaved as domestic servants, wharf hands and craftsmen.

Above: Galveston's east end as seen from the roof of the Hendley building in 1861. *Street Files Collection; courtesy of the Rosenberg Library (Galveston, TX).*

Left: John Sydnor's auction house (demolished), originally located on the north side of the Strand between 22nd and 23rd Streets. *Courtesy of the Galveston Historical Foundation.*

Most African Americans were enslaved for as long as their collective memory reached. Reactions to this unbearable bondage varied. Thousands ran away. Those who witnessed what happened to runaways who were recaptured chose to follow their basic human instinct to survive any way they were able, finding particular strength through religion and the maintenance of their individual cultures as best they could. Randolph B. Campbell, a regents' professor of history at the University of North Texas, noted:

> *Slaves exercised a degree of agency in their lives by maximizing the time available within the system to maintain physical, psychological and spiritual strength. In part, this limited autonomy was given by the masters and was taken by the slaves in the slave quarters which provided them resilience to assert self-determination within the confine of bondage. One way or another they had to endure. This fact is not a tribute to the benevolence of slavery, but a testimony to the human spirit of the enslaved African Americans.*

HISTORIC SIDEBAR
UNDERGROUND RAILROAD SOUTH

Over the years, thousands escaped to Mexico by way of the Underground Railroad South. After the Mexican Congress passed antislavery laws in 1837, enslaved people in Texas, Louisiana, Arkansas and the Territory of Oklahoma became aware of the laws, and as a result, attempts to escape the bondage of slavery increased as enslaved people attempted to reach freedom on the southern side of the Rio Grande River. Mexicans who were working in Texas often befriended enslaved people and assisted them on their southern escape route, while sympathizers along the Texas border of the Rio Grande sometimes helped freedom seekers cross the river. This happened so frequently that enslavers distrusted all Mexicans, and soon, Texas law prohibited Mexicans and enslaved persons from congregating, collaborating or even speaking to each other.

For those who were enslaved on Galveston Island or along the Texas coast, the Gulf of Mexico was the most common path to freedom. Enslaved sailors and stowaways jumped ship

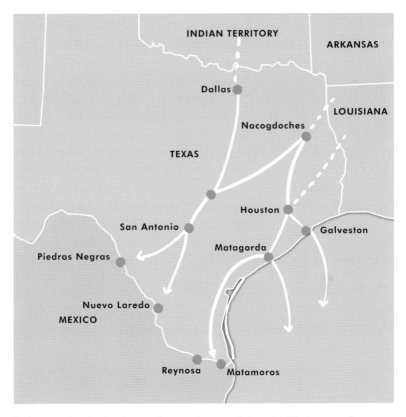

Pathways taken by freedom seekers as they traveled on the Underground Railroad south to Mexico. *Courtesy of the Galveston Historical Foundation.*

in the Mexican ports, yet the majority of escapees from the region traveled by foot over treacherous terrain to cross the river near the Mexican towns of Reynosa, Nuevo Laredo and Piedras Negras. A few rode on horseback, while others who were assigned by their enslavers to drive wagons of cotton to market in Brownsville, Texas, would slip across the muddy waters of the Rio Grande River into Matamoros, Mexico. Rewards for the freedom seekers, with only first names noted, were posted in Texas newspapers with indications that the escapee's destination was south of the border. Some were caught by bounty hunters, and others died before they could reach their destination.

There are few stories that share the lives of those who escaped south, especially when compared to the number of stories from northern escapees like Frederick Douglass, Robert Smalls, Eliza Harris, Henry "Box" Brown, Peter Still, Margaret Garner and William and Ellen Craft. Yet over the years, thousands of enslaved people did manage to escape the bonds of slavery to find freedom in Mexico. Their journey didn't have designated network routes, safehouses or conductors like Harriet Tubman. Life wasn't always perfect in Mexico, but it was much better than the horrific bondage they experienced in the United States. Mexico protected the formerly enslaved from vigilantes and lawmen who crossed the border in their attempts to return escapees to bondage. Their numerous attempts to escape and regain freedom testify to the unbearable cruelty of enslavement.

IN SEPTEMBER 1856, rumors of a nationwide slave insurrection reached Texas. The residents of Columbus, Texas, were the first to act, forming a vigilance committee to investigate the rumors at a local level. They supposedly discovered a plot to murder the White population of the town. The *Galveston News* reported on the committee's discovery of the planned uprising. As a result, the mayor of Galveston, John Henry Brown, called a meeting of the island's slaveholders to discuss a newly adopted resolution concerning the laws that governed slaves and "free negroes" living on Galveston Island.

Mary Madison was one of the "free negroes" who lived on the island. Madison, a free Black nurse living in Galveston before the Civil War, was born in Virginia around 1820. She came to Galveston in 1841 and established a reputation as a valuable citizen, administering healthcare to the community. In 1851, a petition was sent to the Texas legislature on Mary's behalf, asking that she be able to stay in Galveston as a free Black woman. The petition was made in response to an 1840 Republic of Texas law that required free Black people to leave Texas or be sold into slavery. More than eighty White Galvestonians signed the petition, which was approved by the legislature that same year.

TO THE SLAVE-HOLDERS OF GALVESTON.

In pursuance of a Resolution adopted by the City Council, on the 19th of September, the undersigned, as Mayor of the City, respectfully invites the Slave-holders and those controlling slaves in this city, to hold a meeting

At 8 O'clock P. M. at the Mayor's Office,

ON TUESDAY, 30th Inst.

to take into consideration the existing City Laws in regard to slaves and free negroes, that through a Committee, or otherwise, as to them may seem best, they may report to the Council such amendments and modifications as to them shall seem best calculated to preserve order among the negroes, and subserve the best interests of owners, employers and citizens generally.

The Council is desirous of meeting the public wishes on this important subject; and it is hoped there may be a general attendance and full expression of opinion.

Persons wishing copies of the present Laws can get them on application to the undersigned.

JOHN HENRY BROWN,

GALVESTON, Sept. 26, 1856.   *Mayor.*

An 1856 notice to slaveholders. *Courtesy of the Dolph Briscoe Center for American History; University of Texas at Austin.*

An 1851 petition for free Black nurse Mary Madison to remain in Galveston. *Courtesy of the Texas State Library and Archives Commission (Austin, TX).*

HISTORIC SIDEBAR
ANTEBELLUM ARCHITECTURE

The City of Galveston is yet scarcely two years old, and is estimated already to contain from two thousand to twenty-five hundred souls. The houses are framed buildings, most of them painted white, and in their external appearance, resembling the neatest houses of this sort in the small towns of the Eastern States.
 —*"An Account of the Yellow Fever Which Appeared in the City of Galveston, Republic of Texas, in the Autumn of 1839," by Ashbel Smith, MD AM*

The streets are wide and straight, but their cleanliness is about on par with New York, which is not a compliment.
 —*reporter for the* New York Sun, *1847*

The town is flat, rowdy, and drab with houses like "ugly Grecian Boxes with pillars."
 —*a young traveler from Boston, 1859*

Galveston's population remained small in comparison to those of other port cities in the South prior to the Civil War. Despite that, it was Texas's largest urban area and its most sophisticated in terms of its architecture, culture and business. Descriptions by travelers and a few residents recall a town with the majority of the commercial and residential buildings concentrated on the east end near the bay. A number of significant residences of early business leaders, however, were built on outlots on the western edge of the town. Large, imposing, wood-frame, Greek Revival residences and smaller, center-hall, Greek Revival cottages denoted both an accumulation of some personal wealth and traditional building forms and styles common to the South. The red brick construction of Ashton Villa in 1859 indicated the particular wealth of the owners and the initial formation of a boulevard where prominent Galvestonians would begin to build their new homes.

Ashton Villa, designed and constructed between 1855 and 1859, is one of Galveston's most significant properties. The house and attached ancillary buildings were listed in the National Register of Historic Places in 1969. It was built by James Moreau Brown, who moved to Galveston in the 1840s to establish a hardware firm with business partner Henry H. Brower. Their firm, Brown and Bower, noted assets of three enslaved individuals—Austin (thirty-four years old), Sophia and her daughter, Harriet. Austin appears to have been with Brown for only ten years, but Harriet and Sophia continued with the family (enslaved and freed) for the rest of their lives. Sometime before 1850, Brown purchased Aleck, a Black man identified in deed records as being "about 30 years of age, about five-feet-ten inches in height and a brick mason by trade."

In 1855, Brown purchased land on the northeast corner of Broadway Boulevard and 24th Street and began constructing Ashton Villa. The design is attributed to a house plan featured in a book published in 1852 by Philadelphia architect Samuel

Ashton Villa, built in 1859 by James Moreau Brown. Aleck, a brick mason enslaved to Brown, is believed to have been instrumental during its construction. *Courtesy of the Galveston Historical Foundation.*

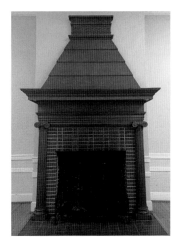

Ashton Villa's family room fireplace, built by Aleck during the 1870s. The fireplace was preserved when the room was enlarged during the 1930s to function as a ballroom. *Courtesy of the Galveston Historical Foundation.*

Sloan titled *The Model Architect.* The source of the brick used in the construction of Ashton Villa is uncertain. As a skilled brick mason, Brown had the training to make the brick himself. However, reputable brick manufacturers existed in the 1850s in Galveston and Houston. The construction of the building was likely led by Aleck. Besides the three-story brick main house, the carriage house and stables were located on the northeast corner. There was room on the second floor where stable hands slept. The third floor was added in the twentieth century, sometime between 1906 and 1912. These buildings were connected by an arcaded walkway to a two-story kitchen behind the house that had quarters on the second level, where Aleck, Sophia and Harriet lived.

After the Civil War ended, Aleck returned as a free man and worked for Brown to construct a family room at the rear of the house that connected the main building to the kitchen. The room included a massive fireplace built by Aleck. In 1899, the house was altered again with an eastern addition to all three floors of the house. Ashton Villa remained in the Brown family until 1927, when it was sold to the El Mina Shrine Temple for use as office space and meeting facilities. The Shriners demolished the Brown family room and kitchen and added the ballroom that is present today. Aleck's fireplace was saved and remains the focal point of the Shriner's ballroom addition.

AFTER ASHTON VILLA WAS COMPLETED, the election of Abraham Lincoln as president in 1860 provoked deep concern in the ranks of the traditional Texas establishment, who were convinced that the labor slavery provided was essential to the economic success of Texas. In 1861, Texas broke away from the Union and joined the Confederate States of America. At the time of the state's annexation, based on the 1860 U.S. slave schedule, at least 30,000 enslaved people lived in Texas. In Galveston, enslaved people numbered 1,178.

Initially, the war had little direct effect within the state, as battles were waged elsewhere. But as the war raged on, the blockade of Texas ports began to take a toll on the Texas economy. Some enslaved people, desperate for freedom, took every opportunity the war offered to flee bondage and escape—initially into Mexico and then, as Union troops closed in on Texas, to their military camps for protection.

During the war, all southern ports were blockaded by the United States fleet, but enforcement was irregular. As a result, Galveston blockade runners maintained the state's ability to transport cotton to Mexico and Cuba before returning to Galveston with military supplies and goods. In 1862, this situation changed when Union forces finally launched a successful assault and occupied the city. However, the island didn't remain under Union control for long.

On New Year's Day 1863, two Confederate river steamers, with a perimeter barricade of cotton bales installed to protect the sharpshooters,

Galveston's Custom House (extant) on the corner of Postoffice and 20th Streets. When completed in 1861, the building was immediately seized by the Confederate army. *Courtesy of the Galveston Historical Foundation.*

The January 1, 1863 Battle of Galveston as depicted in *Harper's Weekly* magazine. *Courtesy of the Texas State Library and Archives Commission (Austin, TX).*

The explosion of the USS *Westfield* during the Battle of Galveston. *Courtesy of the Texas State Library and Archives Commission (Austin, TX).*

Major General Gordon Granger (1821–1876). Granger took command of the District of Texas at the end of the Civil War. *Courtesy of the Library of Congress.*

opened fire at the same time Confederate troops crossed over Galveston Bay from the mainland via an old rail road bridge, and together, the land and sea attack carried the day. The Battle of Galveston is recorded by historians as a largely maritime battle, though some land interaction occurred along 20th Street from Postoffice Street to the former site of Kuhn's Wharf, extending into Galveston Bay from 20th Street. Several hundred men from both the Union and Confederate armies died in the battle, but it lifted the Union blockade of the Port of Galveston. Remnants of the artillery battle still remain along 20th Street, though the battlefield itself is significantly altered today—unlike other Civil War battlefields. After the Confederate victory, the island remained under Confederate occupation until June 1865 and functioned as the only port open in the South for the following years of conflict.

Before the war ended in 1865, Galveston's White population began to return to the island, along with enslaved people who escaped bondage to come to Galveston in search of freedom. By June 1865, everyone awaited the arrival of the Union troops and U.S. Army major general Gordon Granger.

HISTORIC SIDEBAR
THE SLAVE NARRATIVES

The following accounts were taken from *Born in Slavery: Slave Narratives from the Federal Writers' Project, 1936–1938*, which contains more than 2,300 first-person accounts of slavery and 500 black-and-white photographs of formerly enslaved individuals. These narratives were collected in the 1930s as part of the Federal Writers' Project associated with the Works Progress Administration. Historians advise caution, however, as in most cases, the interviewing writers were White, which may have influenced how the formerly enslaved people described their experiences. The accounts were also written from notes and later edited, leading to other areas of possible distortion. Nevertheless, the narratives remain a rich resource to better understand the lived experience of those in slavery. By 1944, the transfer of these interviews to the Library of Congress was completed; they included interviews documented in Texas in 1938 that recorded the recollections of Galveston residents Josephine Riles (sometimes spelled Ryles), Mintie Miller and Amos Sims.

Josephine Williams Riles (1855–1942) was born in Galveston to enslaved parents Mary Alexander and Matt Williams. In her 1937 *Slave Narrative* interview, she recalled her enslaver as James Sultry—most likely James Sorley, a Scottish immigrant who worked as a shipping merchant and insurance agent. Sorley moved from Alabama to Galveston, where 1853 tax records noted he enslaved two people. Riles's mother was from Tennessee but lived in Alabama prior to being brought to Texas. Riles's father, Matt Williams, was enslaved by a man named Schwoebel, and Riles recalled that at the end of the day, when her father's work was done, Mr. Schwoebel allowed him to sleep under the same roof as her and her mother.

When Riles was a toddler, Sorley sold her, her mother and her brother, Charlie Evans, to Polk County residents and plantation owners Thomas and Elvira Snow. Riles's mother cooked for the Snow family, and her brother carried water to the field hands, who numbered more than forty. After Snow died in 1858, probate records for his estate identified Riles's mother as Big Mariah and listed her and her two children as community property valued at $1,200. The three of them managed to stay together until the end of the war, when they returned to Galveston, where Riles hoped to find her father. The reunion was unsuccessful, and she never saw her father again, but in 1878, she began her own family when she married Alex Riles, a laborer and driver for a local lumberyard. The couple and their two daughters, Minnie and Sadie, survived the 1900 storm and remained in Galveston afterward. Alex and Josephine eventually moved in with Sadie and her husband, Frank DeCosta. Josephine assisted Sadie in the birth of her children and then helped raise them after Sadie died in 1924.

Known as Mama Honey to her friends and neighbors, Riles died in Galveston and was buried at Municipal Cemetery with her husband, brother and Sadie. When she was interviewed by Mary E. Liberato in February 1937 for the *Slave Narratives*, Riles vividly recalled the dogs owned by Mr. Snow that hunted down runaways:

> *Plenty of times people run 'way out of de fields. Dey use to work awful hard an' de sun was awful hot, so dey jus' run 'way. De only place dey could go to was de woods an' dey use to hide dere. Mr. Snow use to keep "N***** dogs" to hunt 'em with. Dey was de kind of dogs dat has de big ears. I don' know 'bout 'em. Dey was so bad I never fool 'round 'em. Mr. Snow use to keep 'em chained up 'til one of de field hands run 'way. Den he turn 'em loose to git de scent. Dey kep' on 'til dey found him an' sometimes dey hurt him. I 'member hearin' dem talk 'bout how dey tore de meat off one od de field hands when dey found him. I was 'fraid of 'em. I never went 'round 'em even when dey was chained. Mr. Snow use to whip de field hands when dey caught 'em from runnin' 'way. I never seen no whippin's an' I don' want to. But mostly dey was 'fraid of de dogs.*

Mintie Marie Miller (1852–1938) was born in Alabama and sold to Dr. Massey of Lynchburg, Texas, as a child. Her journey by oxcart to Texas took three months. When freedom

Mintie Marie Miller. *MSS0154-048, Houston Public Library, African American History Research Center.*

Amos Sims. *MSS0154-057, Houston Public Library, African American History Research Center.*

came at the end of the Civil War, Mintie moved to Houston and then to Galveston, where she worked as domestic help for the same family for twenty-four years. During the 1900 storm, Mintie was living with her son, Henry Fields, at 1721 19th Street. She died in Galveston and was buried in Rosewood Cemetery, Galveston's first cemetery designated exclusively for African Americans. When interviewed by Mary E. Liberato on February 2, 1938, for the *Texas Slave Narratives* (vol. 7, part 6), her memories were recorded:

> *I run away when I was a chile lots of times. I couldn't go to my mother, dey didn' 'low me to, so I jus' stay out in de pasture. I never stay out all night. I always come in when it got dark. If dey caught me dey whip me, an' if dey didn' dey didn' whip me. Sometime I run away 'cause somebody made me mad or somethin'. Sometimes I jus' run away for no reason, you know how chillun are. I didn' do no work when I was little. My mother was de cook for de white folks. Dey treated us fine but some of de white folks treated dere slaves awful bad. Dere was a girl in Lynchburg. I can't 'member her name jus' now, she was little, 'bout eight or nine I guess, an' she run 'way from her master. She had to swim de Trinity River an' it was winter an' her feet got frozen. Someone got her an' sold her to a poor white man cheap. He had ten chillun of his own an' he jus' work out for other white folks, He put dis girl's feet in de faire to kind of thaw 'em out and' burn 'em. Well, dere was a law in Lynchburg dat idden you treat a slave like dat dey can take 'em away from you an' sell 'em again. So Dr. Frost took 'er away from dis man an' give 'er to Miss Nancy to take care of 'til she got well. Miss Nancy was de mistress dere at Dr. Massie's place. Dis girl was light, like a Mexican. Miss Nancy wouldn't have any light people. She said dey had white blood in 'em an' she wouldn' have dem. But she said she'd take care of dis girl 'til she got well, so she stay with us.*

Amos Sims (1861–1943) was born on a Texas plantation in Harrison County, Texas, where his parents were enslaved. He married twice in nearby Marion County in 1880 and 1894, and a third marriage to Rosa A. Ways was recorded in Galveston in 1914. It is not known exactly when Amos moved to Galveston, but his first entry in the *Galveston City Directory* was recorded in 1901, when he was noted as a bartender at Lane and Blair, a saloon for African Americans at 2615 Market Street. During his lifetime in Galveston, Amos also worked as a laborer, a porter and, as he got older, a junk dealer. He died in Galveston in April 1943 and was buried in the Municipal Cemetery on 59th Street. During his interview with Mary E. Liberato on March 3, 1937, for the *Texas Slave Narratives* (vol. 9, part 8), his recollection of his father's attempted escape from bondage was recorded:

> *De overseer dere use to whip de colored lots, too. Dey wouldn't let me work, I was too little, but I can 'member lots of whippin's. One time my father run 'way an' hid in de woods. Dey hunt him with dogs dey kep' for huntin' colored folks. Me an' my mother could hear 'em hollerin' an' we cried. Oh, I was jus' a li'l boy den. It took 'em a long time to find 'em, but when dey got 'im dey tied 'im to a post an' whipped 'im. Yes, Ma'm, I 'member dat. He never run 'way no more.*

2

GALVESTON AFTER 1865

Everything in this city seems to be in the utmost confusion as regards the position of the negro. Nobody knows what to do. Many seem to think that all the negroes, young and old, are free to go where they please and that nobody has any right to exercise any control over them but the military authorities.
—*Willard Richardson, editor of the* Galveston Daily News, *June 23, 1865*

The day was abundant in an era of want. Juneteenth planted firm roots within the racial caste system known as Jim Crow....It was a time to reflect on Black progress, but also to remember that the limited version of freedom afforded to African Americans was not what had to be.
—*Brandon Byrd, "The Living History of Juneteenth, Our Next National Holiday,"* GQ *magazine, June 19, 2020*

If the promise of Juneteenth lived anywhere in Texas, it was in Galveston. That sense of promise spread across the state. Black Texans were determined, despite the early intimidating anger of Whites, to celebrate what was initially called Emancipation Day.
—*Annette Gordon-Reed,* On Juneteenth

The Emancipation Proclamation was announced by U.S. president Abraham Lincoln on September 22, 1862. Issued under powers granted to the president "as a fit and necessary war measure," the proclamation declared, "That on the 1ˢᵗ day of January, A.D. 1863, all persons held as

Left: President Abraham Lincoln in February 1864. *Courtesy of the Library of Congress.*

Opposite: Lincoln's Emancipation Proclamation, issued on January 1, 1863. *Courtesy of the Library of Congress.*

slaves within any State or designated part of a State the people whereof shall then be in rebellion against the United States shall be then, thenceforward and forever free."

The Civil War ended in April 1865. Two months later, more than two thousand federal soldiers of the Thirteenth Army Corps arrived and with them Major General Gordon Granger, commanding officer, District of Texas. Granger established his headquarters in the Osterman building, located on the southwest corner of Strand and 22nd Street. It was from this building that General Granger and his chief of staff, Major Frederick Emery, commanded General Orders No. 3 to be posted on June 19, 1865:

The people of Texas are informed that, in accordance with a Proclamation from the Executive of the United States, all slaves are free. This involves an absolute equality of personal rights and rights of property between former masters and slaves, and the connection heretofore existing between them, becomes that between employer and hired labor. The Freedmen are advised to remain at their present homes, and work for wages. They are informed that they will not be allowed to collect at military posts; and that they will not be supported in idleness either there or elsewhere.

The *Galveston News* had little to say about this event other than that Lieutenant Colonel R.G. Laughlin, provost marshal general for Texas, assured the city's mayor that any newly freed people fleeing to Galveston would be "put to work."

Military historian and author Edward T. Cotham noted in his book *Juneteenth: The Story Behind the Celebration* that the enslaved people of Texas

The Osterman building (*left foreground, demolished*), where General Granger established his headquarters after he arrived in Galveston. *Courtesy of the Galveston Historical Foundation.*

learned of their freedom in a number of ways and from a wide variety of sources. Many heard of their freedom from their masters or overseers, who called the enslaved together and made a special announcement. Others learned of their freedom from Union soldiers or other officials sent by the government into the countryside for the express purpose of occupying the state and reestablishing federal authority. Some enslaved people never heard anything about their freedom directly from masters or soldiers; instead, they heard the news indirectly from workers on other farms or passing travelers. Cotham noted:

> *While none of the White inhabitants of Texas should have been surprised by the Juneteenth Order or its contents, many were still caught off-guard by the order. Perhaps the slaveholders were in denial, or perhaps they believed the poisonous editorials in the Texas newspapers that predicted Union soldiers could not and would not carry out the Emancipation Proclamation. Whatever the cause, the Juneteenth Order came as a tremendous shock to many Texans.*

HEAD-QUARTERS DISTRICT OF TEXAS,
GALVESTON, TEXAS, June 19, 1865.

GENERAL ORDERS,
No. 3.

The people of Texas are informed that, in accordance with a Proclamation from the Executive of the United States, all slaves are free. This involves an absolute equality of rights, and rights of property between former master and slaves, and the connection heretofore existing between them becomes that of employer and free laborer. The freedmen are advised to remain at their present homes and work for wages. They are informed that they will not be allowed to collect at Military Posts, and that they will not be supported in idleness, there or elsewhere.

By Order of G. GRANGER, Major General Commanding.

F. W. EMORY, Major and A. A. Gen'l.

Top, left: Granger's commanding officer, General Philip H. Sheridan. *Courtesy of the Library of Congress.*

Top, right: Major Frederick Emery, Granger's assistant adjutant general, drafted and issued the General Orders on behalf of Granger and the U.S. Army. *Courtesy of the Kansas State Historical Society.*

Bottom: General Orders No. 3 enforced Lincoln's 1863 Emancipation Proclamation and announced to the people of Texas that "all slaves are free." *Courtesy of the Library of Congress.*

> Headqrs. Mil. Div of the So. West. New Orleans June 13. 1865.
> To Maej. Gen. Gordon Granger. Comdg 13 Army Corps
> Mobile. Ala.
> On your arrival at Galveston assume command of all the troops in the State of Texas. Carry out the conditions of the surrender of General E Kirby Smith to Maj Gen Canby, notify the people of Texas that in accordance with existing proclamation from the Executive of the United States " That all slaves are free" advise all such freedmen that they must remain at home, that they will not be allowed to collect at military posts, and will not be subsisted in idleness. Notify the people of Texas that all acts of the Governor and Legislature of Texas since the Ordinance of Secession are illigitimate. Take such steps as in your judgement are most conclusive to the restoration of Law and Order, and the return of the State to her true allegiance to the United States Government
> (Signed) P. H. Sheridan.
> Maj Gen Comdg.
>
> Hdqrs. +c
> July 2. 1865
> Official Copy
> (Sp) E B Parsons
> Maj & Asst Adjt Genl.

American historian and law professor Annette Gordon-Reed reflected on the announcement and noted in her book *On Juneteenth* that "the general order announced a state of affairs that completely contravened the racial and economic ideals of the Confederacy. Announcing the end of slavery would have been shocking enough. Stating that the former enslaved would now live in Texas on an equal plane of humanity with Whites was on a different order of magnitude of shocking."

General Orders No. 3 was first read in Galveston, and for many years, its commemoration was a uniquely Texan event. In 1917, the *City Times*

MILITARY ORDERS.

HEAD-QUARTERS U. S. FORCES,
COLUMBUS, TEXAS, June 25, 1865.

IN PURSUANCE of General Order No. 4, from District Head-Quarters, all Arms, Horses, Waggons, Cotton, Munitions of War and Public Property, of every description, belonging to the so-called Government of the Confederate States, or to the State of Texas, will be at once turned in to the Post Quarter Master at this place, under penalty of the arrest of all parties failing to comply with the Order.

L. B. HOUSTON, Maj. 23d Iowa,
Commanding Post.

HEAD-QUARTERS DISTRICT OF TEXAS,
GALVESTON, TEXAS, June 23, 1865.

GENERAL FIELD ORDER.

Columbus, Colorado County, Texas, is designated as a point for the paroling of Prisoners of War surrendered by the Commanding Officer of the Trans-Mississippi Department to the Forces of the United States.

Captain J. M. WALKER, 23d Iowa Vol. Inf., is appointed the Paroling Officer.

By Order of
Major General GRANGER,
WM. L. AVERY, Major and A. D. C.

HEAD-QUARTERS DISTRICT OF TEXAS,
GALVESTON, TEXAS, June 19, 1865.

GENERAL ORDERS,
No. 3.

The people of Texas are informed that, in accordance with a Proclamation from the Executive of the United States, all slaves are free. This involves an absolute equality of rights, and rights of property between former master and slaves, and the connection heretofore existing between them becomes that of employer and free laborer. The freedmen are advised to remain at their present homes and work for wages. They are informed that they will not be allowed to collect at Military Posts, and that they will not be supported in idleness, there or elsewhere.

By Order of
G. GRANGER, Major General Commanding.
F. W. EMORY, Major and A. A. Gen'l.

HEAD-QUARTERS DISTRICT OF TEXAS,
GALVESTON, TEXAS, June 19, 1865.

GENERAL ORDERS,
No. 4.

All acts of the Governor and Legislature of Texas since the Ordinance of Secession are hereby declared illegitimate. All civil and military officers of the so-called Confederate States Government, or of the State of Texas, will at once report for parole at the following places, or such others as may be designated hereafter, to the proper United States Officers, to be appointed: Houston, Galveston, Bonham, San Antonio, Marshall, Brownsville.

Although their long absence from their homes, and the peculiar circumstances of their State may palliate their desertion from their organizations, this Order will be strictly and promptly complied with.

The above-mentioned and all other persons having in their possession public property of any description whatever, as Arms, Horses, Munitions, etc., formerly belonging to the so-called Confederate States, or the State of Texas, will immediately deliver it to the proper United States Officer at the nearest of the above-mentioned places. When they cannot carry it, and have not the means of transporting it, they will make to the same Officer a full report of the character, quantity, location, security, etc. All persons not complying promptly with this Order will be sent North as Prisoners of War, for imprisonment, and their property forfeited. All persons committing acts of violence, such as banditti, guerrillas, jay-hawkers, horse thieves, etc., are hereby declared outlaws, and enemies of the human race, and will be dealt with accordingly.

By Order of
G. GRANGER, Major General Commanding.
F. W. EMORY, Major and A. A. Gen'l.

By order of Gordon Granger
By order of Gordon Granger F. W. Emory Major and A.A. Gen'l

Opposite: A June 13, 1865 letter to Granger from Sheridan outlining the issuance of General Orders 1–5. *Courtesy of the Library of Congress.*

Left: A handbill of military orders that includes General Orders Nos. 2, 3 and 4, issued in Galveston on June 19, 1865. *Courtesy of the Library of Congress.*

observed, "General Granger of the Federal army headquarters at Galveston during the civil war did not make known President Lincoln's famous proclamation until June 19, 1865, and…ever since it has been the custom of our people to celebrate. In no other State in the Union but Texas do the colored people celebrate Juneteenth."

HISTORIC SIDEBAR
THE BIRTH OF JUNETEENTH

A Freedman's Fancy Ball was held at the Berlocher building (2309 Mechanic Street, extant) just a few days after the issuance of General Orders No. 3. It was recorded as one of the first formal celebrations in Galveston, and the city mayor ordered the arrest of the Black promoter of the event the morning after. The mayor's justification for the arrest was that he violated a city ordinance that prohibited public events from being held without permission from city officials. However, the promoter did have permission from Colonel Frederick W. Moore of the Eighty-Third

The Berlocher building, 2309–2315 Mechanic Street (extant), the site of the Freedman's Fancy Ball in January 1866. *Courtesy of the Portal to Texas History, Historic American Building Survey, Texas Historical Commission.*

Ohio Regiment, who released the promotor before he had the mayor arrested and taken to the same jail.

On January 2, 1866, the Galveston newspaper *Flake's Bulletin* reported an emancipation celebration and noted:

> *The colored people of Galveston celebrated their emancipation from slavery yesterday by a procession. Notwithstanding the storm some eight hundred or a thousand men, women and children took part in the demonstration. The procession was orderly and creditable to those participating in it. A meeting was held in the colored Church, on Broadway* [present-day Reedy Chapel], *at which addresses were delivered by a number of speakers, among whom was Gen. Gregory, Assistant Commissioner of Freedmen. The General gave them a great deal of good, plain advice, which, if they follow, will redown to their wellbeing and prosperity. The Emancipation Proclamation of President Lincoln was read. The singing, John Brown's body lies moldering in the ground, was also a part of the programme. So far as we observed there was no interference nor any improper conduct on the part of spectators.*

REEDY'S CHAPEL, GALVESTON, TEXAS.

A depiction of the original sanctuary of Reedy Chapel AME Church. *Courtesy of the Galveston Historical Foundation.*

A band gathers to be photographed at an Emancipation Day celebration in Austin, Texas, in June 1900. *Courtesy of the Austin History Center, Austin Public Library.*

From 1870 to 1900, the number of celebrations reported increased, and they were mainly celebrated on June 19. The traditions of eating watermelon and barbecue at a picnic, wearing fine clothes and enjoying music were established with associations and committees formed to organize the events. In 1872, celebrations were reported thusly:

> *Yesterday, the seventh anniversary of the issuance of the emancipation proclamation in the State, was celebrated by the freedmen with two pic-nics, one at McKinney's and the other at Schmidt's Garden. Both were harmonious and enjoyable occasions for the participants. The processions included several male and female societies in uniform, and they presented a very creditable appearance. The division of the celebration into two parties was caused by a feeling of offended dignity on the part of the McKinney Garden ring, which was averse to the Schmidt Garden privileges being different from those conceded to Whites.*

By 1874, commemorations of emancipation had become even more elaborate, with the procession forming at the

Colored Methodist Church on East Broadway. Led by a band from New Orleans and including representatives from fraternal and commercial organizations as well as youth associations, the parade wound through the city to the picnic grounds. There, celebrants prayed, sang and listened to a reading of the Emancipation Proclamation and several orators. A newspaper account of the festivities concludes, "After enjoying the good things bountifully provided by the female portion of the picnicers, dancing commenced, and was continued until midnight."

After some years of reporting in a flagrantly racist nature, the White Galveston newspapers gradually moved to a less biased accounting of the emancipation celebrations, and by 1878, an anonymous reporter had this to say of the day's celebrants:

> The old plantation melodies…were transformed into a new song and the sunshine of the dreams that once dwelt in their hearts burst full and fair upon them as they both felt and realized the fullness of the freedom that is now theirs—not only to enjoy but to perpetuate….The conclusion of the day went out amid the pleasures that always cluster about the ball-room [sic], and if a memory of olden times came back from the ringing shout of the dancers as the "break-down" was getting the benefit of their "best licks," it is to be hoped that the contrast suggested more of pleasure than regret. The colored people of Galveston certainly deported themselves creditably in celebrating "their 4th of July."

By 1878, when the previous quote was written, the newspaper was also printing wire reports from across the state devoted to emancipation celebrations in Brenham, Marlin, Liberty, Bastrop and elsewhere. African Americans throughout Texas observed June 19 with parades and picnics, speeches and dancing. In many communities, groups bought their own land for these celebrations and other events, often naming these tracts Emancipation Park.

In 1886, the *Galveston Daily News* reported the establishment of a charter for "The Nineteenth of June Emancipation and Historical Association of Galveston." Throughout the

Martha and Pinkie Yates pose for their photograph in a carriage decorated for a Juneteenth celebration in Houston, Texas. *MSS0281-PH038, Houston Public Library, African American History Research Center.*

nineteenth century and into the twentieth century, June 19 was known formally as Emancipation Day, but an item in the *City Times* urged that paper's readers to "spend money with the business houses whose ads appear herein…and be sure and spend your money with them in making purchases for the Juneteenth."

The *City Times*, an African American newspaper published in Galveston, marked Juneteenth each year with reports on large public festivities. One such celebration was held at Crescent Park in LaPorte on Monday, June 20, 1904, and featured a free barbecue for formerly enslaved people, an old fiddler's contest, a Houston-Galveston baseball game, fishing, crabbing, swimming and boat races. Celebrants took advantage of a special excursion train and interurban fares for these giant events, which included the solemnity of the reading of the Emancipation Proclamation and oratory ("Hon. Nat Q. Henderson, grand orator of the day, will address the assembly at 3 p.m.").

Out-of-town excursions were popular in the early years of the twentieth century, although some continued to observe Juneteenth close to home, as seen in this report from 1914: "Galveston came to the front and our people had four different celebrations, the city not being large enough it seems in park facilities. At the McGuire and Cotton Screwmen's park in the city celebrations were held; one at Dickinson, besides one on the Galveston bay on the boat Galvez."

THROUGHOUT THESE YEARS, the *City Times* reported on the social and entertainment aspects of Juneteenth and the Galveston County facilities that provided relaxation and fun for the African American community in the early years of the twentieth century. The newspaper also placed a strong emphasis on the progress African Americans had made since emancipation in articles and editorials detailing their gains in literacy and higher education, business and property ownership and amassed wealth in Galveston, Texas, the South and the nation. In 1917, the paper observed that "recognized authorities of the rise and fall of the human races…cannot help from saying that the Colored American people have made a progress since their freedom that no other people known have been able to round out in little over a half century in the United States."

The *Galveston News* continued to mark Juneteenth observances in much the same manner as the *City Times*, with articles like one in 1923 that stated, "The progress of the negro since the abolition of slavery has been

Flags and bunting draped on a booth at Austin's Emancipation Day celebration in June 1900. *Courtesy of the Austin History Center, Austin Public Library.*

substantial along all lines of human endeavor, to the great credit of the race. In Galveston the advancement has been great."

Also, in the first quarter of the twentieth century, both Black and White newspapers commented on the harmony between the races, particularly the dock workers. The *City Times* stated, "Harmony between [the Black and White laborers] prevails. The colored people of Galveston are well regarded by the white people of the city." Meanwhile, the *Daily News* proclaimed, "These laborers work with a harmonious spirit of friendliness and brotherhood not to be equaled at any other seaport in the country."

3

RECONSTRUCTION IN GALVESTON

1865–1900

The war may not have brought a great deal of bloodshed to Texas,
but the peace certainly did.
—*Elizabeth Hayes Turner, historian, University of Texas*

In 1867, an engraving titled *Reconstruction: Bateman's National Picture*, by J.L. Giles, appeared in the American magazine *Harper's Weekly*. The engraving presented a grand allegory of the reconciliation between the North and the South through the federal program of Reconstruction. The optimism represented in the engraving was belied by many setbacks, as White Texans found ways to erode both the reconstruction and the actual freedom of African Americans, who became subject to increasing violence from the White population.

Despite these setbacks, African Americans nourished their freedom and struggled to build new lives in the face of opposition in many quarters. In 1867, a group of Black cowboys, some of whom were previously enslaved on the Butler Ranch in north Galveston County, established the only Reconstruction-era community in Galveston County. Located in Texas City and known today as the 1867 Settlement, their community maintained its identity and distinctive presence for over one hundred years. Others struggled through the nineteenth and twentieth centuries, and despite many breakthroughs over time, challenges persist today and are the reason the Galveston Historical Foundation's African American Heritage Committee chose the title *And Still We Rise*.

A Reconstruction lithograph published by Horatio Bateman in 1867. *Courtesy of the Library of Congress.*

SOCIAL FABRIC OF GALVESTON

In 1865, the Freedmen's Bureau was established as a branch of the army to assist African Americans in the South with their transition to freedom.

HISTORIC SIDEBAR
THE FREEDMEN'S BUREAU

As the Civil War was ending, on March 3, 1865, the United States Congress passed "An Act to establish a Bureau for the Relief of Freedmen and Refugees" with a mission to provide food, shelter, clothing, medical services, land and an overall smooth transition into the social system for all displaced Southerners, both the newly freed African Americans as well as White Southerners. The organization was originally known as the Bureau of Refugees, Freedmen and Abandoned Lands, and President Abraham Lincoln approved the act and gave the new bureau a charter for one year.

After President Lincoln was assassinated by James Wilkes Booth, Vice President Andrew Johnson assumed the presidency. Johnson believed the work of restoring the Union was completed and that the Freedmen's Bureau was no longer necessary. When Congress renewed the bureau's charter in 1866, Johnson vetoed the measure on the grounds that it interfered with the states' rights. To retaliate, Congress overturned Johnson's veto.

On May 12, 1865, Major General Oliver O. Howard was appointed the chief commissioner for the Freedmen's Bureau and served as the agency's only commissioner until the bureau was dismantled by Congress in 1872. Under his leadership, the bureau's territory was divided into twelve districts, and in September 1865, he appointed General E.M. Gregory as assistant commissioner for Texas. Gregory arrived in Galveston on September 21, 1865, and began to organize the Texas district, covered by twelve local agents, including five civilians.

The Freedmen's Bureau lithograph by artist A.R. Waud, published in July 1868. *Courtesy of the Library of Congress.*

The Barnes Institute, established in 1869. The school was located on Avenue M between 28th and 29th Streets. *G-files: Education Collection, courtesy of the Rosenberg Library (Galveston, TX).*

In addition to providing relief work and court protection, the bureau also organized schools for the newly freed Black citizens with Lieutenant E.M. Wheelock, a member of the United States Colored Troops who was assigned the role of educational director for Texas.

Financed by bureau funds, White missionary Sarah Barnes opened Galveston's Barnes Institute in September 1865 as the first school for African Americans in Galveston. Alfred Perkins, one of Galveston's earliest African American settlers after the Civil War, provided the needed land and aided the building's construction. The school was a success, and soon, more schools were established in other Texas towns. By January 1866, Lieutenant Wheelock reported 14 teachers led classes for 1,691 students enrolled across the state. The schools operated on volunteer contributions and an annual tuition of $1.50 per student.

Along with education, land management was another concern for the Freedmen's Bureau. The bureau was in control of all abandoned and confiscated lands, which were sold for a small price to encourage landownership among the freedmen.

When Brevet Major General J.B. Kiddoo was chosen to succeed General Gregory, most Texans welcomed the change with hopes that Kiddoo would do more to relieve congestion in cities by influencing the freedmen to return to the rural settings and farms where they previously lived.

Congress later decided that no ex-Confederates' land could be given or sold to the freedmen, so many were expelled from land they had paid for. After these freedmen lost their property, the bureau encouraged them to work for former enslavers. Many became tenant farmers, while others ended up renting from former enslavers who took advantage of them and often denied them their earnings.

In 1868, the Freedmen's Bureau was phased out in Texas. Some African Americans who worked for the Freedmen's Bureau later became Texas delegates and legislators, including George Ruby of Galveston, Jeremiah Hamilton of Bastrop and Richard Allen of Houston.

ON JUNE 8, 1866, the Fourteenth Amendment became law and granted citizenship to all persons "born or naturalized in the United States." The amendment included citizenship for formerly enslaved people and provided all citizens with "equal protection under the laws." The Texas Constitutional Congress refused to ratify the Fourteenth Amendment, which granted citizenship and equal civil and legal rights to African Americans. Instead, in 1866, Texas legislators passed laws that become known as the Black Codes.

HISTORIC SIDEBAR
THE BLACK CODES

Very similar to the prewar slave codes, the Eleventh Texas Legislature implemented the Black Codes in an attempt to maintain political dominance and suppress the new freedmen

An 1866 "Slavery Is Dead" lithograph. *Thomas Nast, artist; courtesy of the Library of Congress.*

by confirming the subordinate position of free Black people and regulated Black labor. The codes made it clear that White people were not willing to accept Black people as equals and perpetuated their fears that freed people would not work unless there were specific laws in place. The language used in the last sentence of General Orders No. 3—"They are informed that they will not be allowed to collect at military posts and will not be supported in idleness either there or elsewhere"—indicated this inequality would continue. This perhaps gave some leverage in writing the laws that imposed a variety of restrictions on African Americans. Under the code, African Americans were not allowed to vote, hold office or serve on juries. Interracial marriage was outlawed. The segregation of the races was imposed on railroad cars, and state support for public land use and educational institutions for African Americans was barred.

The Black Codes also defined labor relations and allowed local courts to arrest individuals deemed idle to impose monetary fines on them and then apply mandatory work details if they could not pay the fines. Employers had the power to deduct an employee's wages if they were believed to be guilty of theft or disobedience, if they missed work without permission or were accused of destroying property. Persons under the age of twenty-one could be apprenticed with parental consent or by order of a county court. Employers were also given permission to impose corporal punishment on any apprentice who refused to work. Physical punishment was allowed.

Peonage, another system of holding one in bondage, occurred when employers compelled employees to pay off their debts owed with manual labor. In most cases, the debt was difficult to pay off, and workers found themselves in a continuous cycle of working without pay. This also resulted in their indebtedness to merchants as well or for any other service provided. The system of sharecropping was also a form of peonage. Although the city of Galveston didn't have the rich soil necessary to produce cash crops, communities on the mainland produced cotton, sugarcane and other crops. Freedmen who wanted to earn wages and landowners who needed workers supported the sharecropping system, in which landowners allowed freed people to work the land and were given a share of the profits reaped from harvest. In many cases, landlords leased equipment to these workers and offered other items on credit until the harvest. When it was time for workers to receive their wages, high interest rates, unpredictable harvests and dishonest planters and merchants found ways to keep payments at a minimum. Workers were offered loans against the next harvest, which kept them in debt and continued the ruthless cycle.

TEXAS EVENTUALLY RATIFIED the Fourteenth Amendment in 1870, but for many years, courts largely failed to enforce it. The first Texan election in which African American men were entitled to participate resulted in ten African American delegates being elected. Among them was George T. Ruby of Galveston, who went on to serve in the Texas legislature from 1870 to 1874. Ruby left Louisiana in September 1866 after being beaten by a White mob while trying to establish a common school in Jacksboro. He joined the Freedmen's Bureau in Galveston and began administering the bureau's schools. He also taught school at the Methodist Episcopal Church.

Left: Educator and statesman George Ruby. *Courtesy of the Texas State Library and Archives Commission (Austin, TX).*

Right: Major General Charles Griffin appointed Galveston's first Black policemen in 1867. *Courtesy of the Library of Congress.*

The Freedmen's Bureau's records show that from 1865 to 1868, White Texans committed some 2,000 acts of violence against African Americans and murdered over 370 of them. Newly established African American schools were frequent targets, with more than 631 school burnings recorded between 1864 and 1876, of which 57 occurred in Texas. The Freedman's Bureau attempted to curb this violence, but in an increasingly hostile environment, these efforts were reduced over the years.

During the Reconstruction period that followed the end of the Civil War, Texas was occupied by Union forces from 1867 to 1873. On June 8, 1867, Major General Charles Griffin, while stationed in Galveston, was not pleased with the performance of the local police and instructed Mayor James E. Haviland to dismiss the entire police force. General Griffin then submitted to the mayor his own list of officers, which included the names of "five colored men." The mayor challenged the general in his selection of these five Black officers, and after several communications and meetings, General Griffin dismissed the mayor and appointed Isaac G. Williams as the new mayor. The June 9, 1867 issue of the *Galveston Daily News* listed the first Black police officers in Galveston: William Easton, Anderson Hunt, Simon Malone, Solomon Riley and Robert Smith.

HISTORIC SIDEBAR
EARLY PUBLISHERS AND ACTIVISTS

The city's first Black publisher, Richard Nelson (1842–1914), produced the first issue of his newspaper the *Representative* on May 22, 1871. The Galveston periodical was the first newspaper in Texas owned, edited and published by an African American. Nelson was born in Key West, Florida, and moved to Galveston in 1866. His political career began in 1869, when he ran for the Texas legislature as a Republican. Unsuccessful in his campaign, he became a justice of the peace for Galveston County the next year. In 1871, he represented Texas at the Washington convention of the National Labor Union, where he served on several committees. Upon his return to Galveston, he organized a state labor meeting and ran unsuccessfully for the Republican nomination in Congress. In 1873, Nelson established the weekly newspaper the *Galveston Spectator*. Both the *Galveston Spectator* and the *Representative* were important early printed platforms for the Black community.

In 1880, Nelson served as secretary for the Republican state convention. Four years later, he ran as an independent Republican for the United States House of Representatives but was defeated. During the 1880s, Nelson worked as an inspector for the Federal Customs Office in Galveston and was appointed postmaster for the post office on Virginia Point. He returned to journalism in 1887 with the *Freeman's Journal*, which continued until 1893. Nelson also published letters in the Indianapolis, Indiana, *Freeman* periodical concerning political discrimination and lynching. In 1901, Nelson was elected vice-president of the Southern Negro Congress, an organization focused on the economic and educational advancement for African Americans.

Newspaper publisher William Henry Noble (1873–1930) was born in Woodville, Wilkinson County, Mississippi, to Eloise Harris. Harris and her parents, William and Caroline, and three sisters were enslaved by Carnot Posey, a Mississippi lawyer, planter and Confederate general from Woodville. Noble's 1930 death certificate noted his father's name as William Henry Noble—most likely a Woodville native and sheriff of Wilkinson County, as well as the publisher of the *Woodville Republican* from 1869 to 1876. The antebellum Woodville homesteads of the Noble and Posey families are located two blocks apart on Church Street.

Newspaper publisher William Henry Noble. *Name Files Photograph Collection, courtesy of Rosenberg Library (Galveston, TX).*

The Harris family left Woodville soon after Noble's birth and relocated to Galveston. Noble's first entry in the *Galveston City Directory* came in 1890–91, when he was noted as a clerk for African American grocer George Ashe and, later, at William Lane's African American restaurant located at 507 24th Street. In 1895, the *Galveston City Directory* recorded Noble's employment as city editor for the *Galveston Witness*, an African American newspaper published by John S. Tibbett. By 1897, the directory noted Noble as the editor and proprietor of the *Galveston City Times*, a weekly newspaper for African Americans edited and published by Noble until 1927. Noble resided at 1309 Avenue L with his wife, Irene Lockhart, and their six children. Their youngest daughter, Eleanor Noble Gordon (1914–1988), became a distinguished Galveston educator whose career spanned over forty years.

In addition to publishing a newspaper in Galveston, Noble was a political and community activist who promoted Negro Children and Old Folk's Day, a popular event hosted annually, and held leadership positions with the Young Men's Republican League, the Anti-Lynching Society, the Southern Negro Congress and the Negro Board of Trade, which evolved into the Negro Chamber of Commerce. Led by Noble as chairman and, later, president, the commercial group held regular meetings at Progress Hall, built by the Loyal Knights of Progress in 1922 (2609 Avenue L, extant).

Activist, politician and union leader Norris Wright Cuney (1846–1898) improved education for African Americans in Galveston and established a union for Galveston's Black dockworkers. Cuney was born near Hempstead, Texas, to a prominent White plantation owner and an enslaved mother. Educated in Pennsylvania, Cuney traveled around the United States during the Civil War and eventually settled in Galveston, where he studied law and became a well-known figure in Texas and at the national level. During his life, Cuney served as city alderman and was appointed a school director in Galveston County in 1871. He was the first grand master of the Prince Hall Masons in Texas from 1875 to 1877 and founded the local chapter for African Americans in 1871. In 1872, Cuney became the special inspector of customs in Galveston and eventually the collector of customs for the port in 1889.

In 1879, Cuney was asked to lead the newly formed Cotton Jammers Association, a group of African American longshoremen who were denied entry into the Screwmen's Benevolent Association, a group of specialized longshoremen who, with the aid of a tool called a screwjack packed cotton into the holds of ships. Cuney organized the Screwmen's Benevolent Association no. 2 in 1883 and, on orders from a federal judge, the Black chapter and another African American ILA local were later merged with two White ILA locals.

Cuney held several positions with the Republican Party, including secretary of the State Executive Committee, first assistant to the sergeant-at-arms of the twelfth state legislature and, eventually, the position of chairman of the Texas Republican Party, where he became a national committeeman. He was a delegate to the Republican Party National Conventions from 1872 to 1892 and ran for mayor of Galveston and the state senate but was defeated in both elections. His role

Activist and politician Norris Wright Cuney. *Courtesy of Old Central Cultural Center Inc.*

with the Republican Party presented him with opportunities to improve the lives of African Americans in Galveston and the rest of Texas. Today, the Wright Cuney Recreational Center at 718 41st Street honors his memory.

In addition to Cuney, D.H. "Doc" Hamilton (1870–1939) held several positions with the International Longshoremen's Association Local no. 851, including president. Hamilton was the first African American to be elected to the executive board of the South Atlantic and Gulf Coast District of the International Longshoremen's Association.

RELIGIOUS LIFE

Several of the first churches for African Americans in the state of Texas were established in Galveston. Reedy Chapel African Methodist Episcopal, first noted as the "Negro Church on Broadway"; Avenue L Missionary Baptist; Holy Rosary Catholic; and St. Augustine of Hippo Episcopal represent the four oldest Black churches in Texas.

Avenue L Baptist Church (2612 Avenue L) was started in 1840, when Galveston's newly formed First Baptist Church organized a church for its enslaved population. Called the Colored Baptist Church, it initially had just five members. In the 1850s, the church became known as the African Baptist Church and was housed in a building located at 26th Street and Avenue L. Reverend Israel L. Campbell reorganized the congregation as the First Regular Missionary Baptist Church in 1867.

In 1891, a new building arose on Avenue L, only to be badly damaged by the 1900 storm. The church was rebuilt, and its present name, Avenue L Baptist Church, was also adopted. By 1915, the congregation had outgrown the new church, and in 1916, Tanner Brothers Contractors and Architects, an African American firm, laid the cornerstone for the present building on January 7, 1917. In 1982, Avenue L Baptist Church was designated a Recorded Texas Historical Landmark.

Reedy Chapel African Methodist Episcopal Church (2015 Broadway) was established in 1848, when parishioners and trustees of Galveston's Methodist Episcopal Church South decided to form a church for their

Avenue L Baptist Church, 2612 Avenue L, founded in 1840. *Courtesy of the Galveston Historical Foundation.*

enslaved population under the Methodist Episcopal bishop. Trustees purchased property at Broadway and 20th Street for that purpose, and later, a church building and parsonage were erected and given to the enslaved as the Negro Methodist Episcopal Church South.

The Negro Methodist Episcopal South was reorganized in 1866 as the first African Methodist Episcopal Church in Texas and turned over to its Black membership on March 13, 1867. The church was later renamed Reedy Chapel after the Reverend Houston Reedy, the second pastor of the church. In 1885, a fire that destroyed forty square blocks of Galveston burned the 1848 church. A year later, the present Reedy Chapel AME Church was built. Norris Wright Cuney, a Reedy parishioner, laid the masonry. The first two annual conferences of the African Methodist Episcopal Church held in Texas were hosted by Reedy in 1867 and 1868. The building, designed by architect Benjamin G. Chisolm, was placed in the National Register of Historic Places in 1984.

St. Augustine of Hippo Episcopal Church (1410 41st Street) was first organized in 1884 at the urging of Black seamen from the West Indies. A temporary chapel was located at 15th Street and Avenue L and utilized for services until 1889, when the church purchased property on the southeast corner of Broadway and 22nd Street. During the 1900 storm, the church and

Right: The current sanctuary of Reedy Chapel AME Church at 2015 Broadway was built after the original church was destroyed by fire in 1885. *Courtesy of the Galveston Historical Foundation.*

Below: Holy Rosary African American Catholic Church, 1420 31st Street, organized in 1889. *Courtesy of the Galveston Historical Foundation.*

Opposite: Saint Augustine of Hippo Episcopal Church, 1410 41st Street, organized in 1884. *Courtesy of the Galveston Historical Foundation.*

rectory were literally washed away. Eighteen months later, a campaign was held to rebuild several Episcopal churches destroyed in the great storm, and a loan was secured to rebuild St. Augustine on the site of the former church. A new building was consecrated on St. Thomas' Day 1902. The building was cut in half in 1940 and moved to its present site at 1410 41st Street.

In 1886, the Most Reverend Nicholas Gallagher, bishop of the Roman Catholic Diocese of Galveston (now Galveston-Houston), established the first African American Catholic school in Texas in a cottage at the corner of 12th Street and Avenue K. Organized as part of Holy Rosary African American Catholic Church, Holy Rosary Industrial School taught dressmaking, cooking and housekeeping to African American children. In 1914, the church and its associated buildings were moved from the original site at 25th Street and Avenue L to the present location on Avenue N between 30th and 31st Streets (1420 31st Street). A high school curriculum was added to the school in 1927, and it became the first accredited Catholic high school for Black students in Texas. The current church building was constructed in 1950.

Other historic African American congregations formed in Galveston include St. Paul United Methodist (1425 Broadway, organized 1866), Wesley Tabernacle United Methodist (902 28th Street, organized 1869), Shiloh African Methodist Episcopal (1310 29th Street, organized 1870), West Point Missionary Baptist (3009 Avenue M, organized 1870), First Union Missionary Baptist (1027 Avenue K, founded 1870), Mount Olive Missionary Baptist (3602 Sealy Street, organized 1876), Mount Pilgrim Missionary Baptist (3215 Broadway, organized 1883), Macedonia Missionary Baptist (2920 Avenue M½, formed 1889), St. Luke Missionary Baptist (1301 Avenue L, formed 1894) and Trinity Missionary Baptist (1223 32nd Street, now Bethel Baptist Church).

EDUCATIONAL ADVANCES

With funds made available from the Freedmen's Bureau, White missionary Sarah Barnes established the Barnes Institute in 1869, the first school for African Americans in Galveston. The school was located on Avenue M between 28th and 29th Streets. John Ogilvie Stevenson, a native of Scotland, served with the American Missionary Association and was the school's first principal. George Thompson Ruby (1841–1882) was the bureau's administrator of schools and one of the institute's first instructors. Born in New York City and educated in the public schools of Portland, Maine, Ruby moved to Louisiana in 1864 to accept a teaching position. Two years later, as he attempted to establish a school for Black students in Jacksboro, a White mob forced him to leave. Ruby relocated to Galveston County and joined the Freedman's Bureau as the administrator of schools. In addition to his administrative and teaching duties, Ruby was a correspondent for the *New Orleans Tribune*, taught classes at the African Methodist Episcopal Church on Broadway (Reedy AME), established Galveston's first labor union for Black men and served as deputy customs collector for the Port of Galveston from 1869 to 1872.

Ruby was an active participant in the Texas Republican Party with substantial influence on both the White and Black members of the party. In 1868, a group of predominantly White supporters elected him as a delegate to the State Constitutional Convention, and in 1869, he was elected to the Texas Senate. As a member of the twelfth and thirteenth legislature, Ruby demonstrated strong leadership skills and introduced bills important to Galveston, the economic development of Texas and the establishment of the Texas militia.

By 1876, Ruby had returned to Louisiana and left the campus of the Barnes Institute with four teachers and an enrollment of more than three hundred students. Frank Webb became principal in 1881 and served until 1894. During his tenure, the school grew significantly and was renamed the West District Colored School. The West District School, located on Winnie Street, between 27th and 28th Streets, was an elementary school for African American children who lived west of 20th Street. By 1890, the school had relocated to the south side of Avenue M, between 28th and 29th Streets. A second elementary school for African American children living east of 25th Street was established in 1871. The East District School was located on the north side of Broadway, between 9th and 10th Streets.

Central High School, organized in 1885, was the first high school for African Americans in Texas. Classrooms were initially housed in a rented building located at 16th Street and Avenue L. From 1886 to 1893, the school was operated from a second location at 15th Street and Avenue N. In 1893,

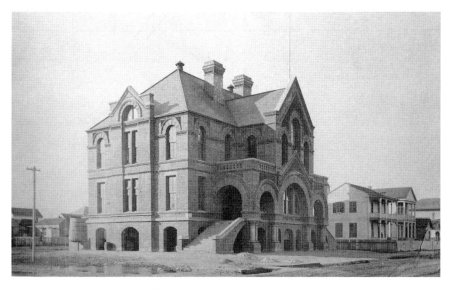

The third campus of Central High School, erected in 1893 and designed by Nicolas J. Clayton. The building was located on the southwest corner of 26th Street and Avenue M. *Courtesy of the Galveston Historical Foundation.*

The existing entrance over the African American branch of Rosenberg Library, opened in 1905 on the campus of Central High School. *Courtesy of the Galveston Historical Foundation.*

land was purchased between 26th and 27th Streets on Avenue M for a new school designed by the notable Galveston architect Nicholas Clayton. The handsome brick building was the third campus for Central High School. As the student body at Central High School grew, a new wing was added in 1924 to increase the number of classrooms needed for the growing enrollment. As a result of collaborations between the all-White Rosenberg Library Association, the Galveston School Board and the City of Galveston, an addition of a public library at Central High School was authorized on May 18, 1904. In January 1905, the Colored Branch of the Rosenberg Library became the first African American public library in Texas. The final Central High School was built in 1954 and spanned from 31st to 32nd Streets between Avenues H and I (3014 Sealy Street, extant).

HISTORIC SIDEBAR
JOHN R. GIBSON

John Rufus Gibson (1865–1948) was the first principal of Central High School. Appointed in 1886, Gibson held the position until 1936. Born in Loudoun County, Virginia, Gibson graduated from Ohio's Wilberforce University in 1882 and came to Galveston soon after. In Galveston, he joined Wilberforce classmate Felix H. Mabson (1856–1890), the principal of Galveston's East District School on Broadway. Gibson and Mabson were among the original founders of the Colored Teachers State Association of Texas, formed in 1885. Gibson's educational career continued for more than fifty years with one temporary leave of absence in 1901, when President William McKinley appointed him consular general of Monrovia, Liberia. Gibson held that position for several years before he returned to his duties at Central High School. Gibson was a member of the NAACP, the president of the Relief Association (established to assist the elderly) and a facilitator of a local Boy Scout troop and YMCA branch for Galveston's African American youth, the latter of which still carries his name.

MEDICAL PIONEERS

Before freedom arrived in Galveston on June 19, 1865, with the reading of General Orders No. 3, enslaved people who required medical care were taken care of by their enslavers. After the war ended, the African American citizens of Galveston, who came from the plantations of Matagorda County, Brazoria County and southern Louisiana, received medical treatment in their homes or in segregated areas in the hospitals called "colored wards." Although there were wards in the White hospitals for Black patients, African American doctors could not practice in these hospitals.

When the Civil War began, at least ten medical schools located in northern states accepted African American applicants. When the war ended, fourteen medical schools were established for African Americans. Two of the most well attended were Howard University and Meharry Medical College. Howard was established in 1867 in Washington, D.C., and was named for the commissioner of the Freedman's Bureau. The school was established primarily to help freed slaves. Meharry Medical College was established in 1876 in Nashville, Tennessee, by the Methodist Episcopal Church and the Freedman's Aid Society. Between 1910 and

1947, Howard and Meharry accounted for 90 percent of the African American medical school graduates.

In 1882, in Austin, Texas, Dr. Quinton B. Neal became the first African American physician to practice medicine in the state. Four years later, in August 1886, in the office of Galveston doctors and brothers J.H. and L.M. Wilkins, a meeting was called to order. Along with J.S. Cameron, a San Antonio pharmacist, twelve Black doctors from nine towns, including Dr. Benjamin Jessie Covington (1869–1961), the son of former slaves, established the Lone Star Medical Association in response to the men's denied admission to the all-White Texas Medical Association.

Dr. Benjamin Jessie Covington, one of the founders of the Lone Star State Medical, Dental and Pharmaceutical Association. *MSS2001-70-001, Houston Public Library, African American History Research Center.*

The first African American medical association in the state of Texas and the second in the nation, their association was later known as the Lone Star State Medical, Dental and Pharmaceutical Association. After the 1900 storm, Dr. J.H. Wilkins moved to Houston before he settled in Victoria, Texas. In his later years, Wilkins treated patients of all races at his Victoria office.

HISTORIC SIDEBAR
DRS. JOHN H. AND LEWIS M. WILKINS

John Henry Wilkins, MD (1853–1917), was born in Georgia and graduated from Meharry Medical College in 1880. In 1884, Wilkins was the first Black physician to present a certificate to the Galveston County Clerk from the Examining Board of the Sixth Judicial District in a request to open a medical practice in the city. Initially located at 316 25th Street and later 420 22nd Street, Wilkins's practice thrived. His brother, Lewis Melton Wilkins, MD (1859–1928), an active member within the community as well as the state, entered the Galveston medical practice after he graduated from Meharry College in 1887. His nephew George Melton Wilkins, MD (1890–1969), took over the Galveston practice after he passed the Kentucky medical examination during his junior year at Meharry College and made the Wilkins firm the first second-generation Black medical practice in Texas.

4

JIM CROW ERA

1900–1961

Slavery was just a blink of an eye away from the years my grandparents and their friends were born. Although I was angered by the stories I heard about their lives under Jim Crow…they surely compared life as it was, knowing what it could have been but for the Civil War, the Emancipation Proclamation, and General Orders No. 3.
—*Annette Gordon-Reed,* On Juneteenth

The period immediately after the 1900 storm was difficult for African Americans in Galveston. They lost all political influence, as oppression steadily grew not only locally but also across the state of Texas and the South, where Jim Crow laws were rampant. In 1905, a city ordinance was passed to segregate the streetcars. There were no public places in Galveston where African Americans could sit next to White people. The growing prejudice against Black people did not halt the growth of economic progress within the Black community. Cotton was the driving force of economic growth in both White and African American communities, and many of the members of the Wesley Tabernacle congregation were also members of the Cotton Jammer's Association and the Screwmen's Benevolent Association no. 2, organized by Norris Wright Cuney.

In 1909, the *City Times* listed the following demographics for the African American community: annual income in salaries, $332,514; over one thousand Black men employed at the wharves; seventy-five Black-owned

Left: A gang of cotton jammers screw cotton into the hold of a ship in Galveston's harbor. *Courtesy of the New York Public Library.*

Below: A cotton truck bound for the waterfront leaves a warehouse loaded with bales in 1926. *Courtesy of the Galveston Historical Foundation.*

businesses; four Black physicians; four Black attorneys; twenty-three Black teachers and administrators; and sixteen Black clergymen. As bigotry and prejudice grew around the state, the lynching of Black men became more common. In response, members of Wesley Tabernacle Church organized the first Anti-Lynching Society in Texas in 1914. African American churches had become the safe harbor for Black political growth.

Rosewood Cemetery
2825 63ʳᴰ Street

At Wesley Tabernacle Methodist Church in 1911, a group of African Americans met to establish the Rosewood Cemetery Association. In earlier years, African Americans had purchased burial plots in Lakewood Cemetery in a special section dedicated to them. Some African Americans were able to purchase plots in White cemeteries, but the only other place for African Americans to be buried was the New Potters Field located on the outskirts of town. W.S. Chinn, the pastor of the church, told the group that "a site has been offered to the colored people consisting of 8½ acres for $1,000 or $1,200. An organization consisting of 40 people who would pledge themselves to pay $30 apiece should be formed."

Those in attendance voted to form the organization. The association purchased land south of the beach accessed from 61ˢᵗ Street from the Joe Levy family. Ownership was divided among eighty-six shares with twenty-six shareholders. The first burial here was that of Robert Bailey on February 1, 1912; the last burial was that of Frank Boyer on June 29, 1944. The association provided guidelines for the grave coverings, and some of the original curbing exists in tile form and could represent cultural/tribal affiliation. Most of the identified headstones date from 1914 and 1915. Out of the 411 burials that took place at Rosewood, the exact number of plots remaining on the 1.255 acres is still unknown. Recent surveys identified only 20 remaining grave markers.

Recorded minutes show grave sites were sold for ten dollars, plus two dollars for grave digging for those over twelve years of age. Early burials in Rosewood Cemetery were serviced by Columbus S. Willis. Born in Shreveport, Louisiana, Willis came to Galveston around 1910 or 1911 and established his funeral home and funeral supply company. In 1911, Willis was the only African American undertaker listed in the *Galveston City Directory*. Although African Americans operated virtually every kind of business during the late nineteenth and early twentieth centuries, some of the most prominent Black-owned businesses were funeral parlors, as it was considered illegal for a White undertaker to handle a Black corpse. In addition to his funeral parlor, Willis served as president of the Rosewood Cemetery Association, with J.W. Smith (secretary) and J.O. Williams as board members. In 1916, the business became Willis and Herbert when William Herbert returned home from World War I and joined Willis as a partner.

Rosewood Cemetery, established in 1911, was Galveston's first cemetery designated for African Americans. *Courtesy of the Galveston Historical Foundation.*

On September 7, 1945, Wright Cuney Lodge no. 63, one of the cemetery shareholders, executed a document to sell its shares to Thomas Armstrong. Armstrong represented the County of Galveston for the seawall extension project. In 1951, Galveston County purchased a large portion of land from the Rosewood Cemetery Association. Armstrong purchased the remaining shares in 1957. In 1980, Armstong's estate sold the land, which was later donated to the Galveston Historical Foundation.

Rosewood Cemetery is significant in Galveston's history, as it was the first burial ground designated for African Americans on the island. A number of prominent African Americans were buried at the cemetery, with a sizable number of them having been leaders and workers who held lifelong positions on the wharves of the Port of Galveston. The labor organization that was formed for those workers provided them an opportunity to improve their lives and economic positions, thus allowing them to buy plots in Rosewood. Rosewood Cemetery holds the burial plots of World War I veterans and many victims from the hurricane of 1915. Based on extensive research conducted by Tommie Boudreaux, a Texas Historical Commission subject marker for Rosewood Cemetery provides a layer of education and interpretation to visitors about Galveston's rich African American history.

GHF's African American Heritage Committee at the state marker dedication for Rosewood Cemetery in 2011. *Courtesy of the Galveston Historical Foundation.*

Theodore Patrick (*top right*) with Galveston's "Four Minute Men." The men spoke publicly in support of the United States' involvement in World War I. The group included Dr. R.H. Stanton and Rufus Gibson. *Courtesy of the R.H. Stanton family.*

Other members of Wesley Tabernacle who went on to dedicate their lives to the betterment of Galveston's Black community were Theodore W. and Mary A. Patrick. T.W. Patrick was a postman, prominent civic leader and lay member of Wesley Tabernacle and the Texas Conference of the Methodist Church. He served on local interracial committees, chaired the T.W. Patrick Division of the Bay Area Council of Boy Scouts of America and held a position on the board of directors for the Gibson branch of the YMCA. Patrick also served as a trustee of Wiley College in Marshall, Texas, and was the treasurer of the Knights of Pythias for the State of Texas. Mary Patrick was one of the founders of the Mary Patrick branch of the YWCA for African American girls and a member of the Ever Ready Charity Club, which was founded in 1919 to provide care as well as burial arrangements for indigent and elderly women of color.

HISTORIC SIDEBAR
CHARITABLE ORGANIZATIONS: MARYS HOME FOR AGED NEGRO WOMEN AND MRS. YEAGER'S DAY NURSERY AND KINDERGARTEN

In 1921, Ever Ready Charity Club trustees Mary Patrick, Mamie L. Kemp and Mary L. Rogers purchased a two-story house at 2823 Avenue K for use as a home for indigent and elderly African American women. Named Marys Home for Aged Colored Women, the first home was opened on the corner of 39th Street and Avenue O½ in 1917. A larger house was purchased in 1921 that enabled the group to double the number of residents it cared for. The group operated through donations and funding received from Galveston County and the Community Chest. At least two residents of Marys Home, Eliza Beecham and Lue Phillips, were later interred at Rosewood Cemetery.

Kemp served as matron of the home until her death in 1930. Rogers assumed the role after Kemp's death and also served on the boards of the Negro Board of Trade and Negro Chamber of Commerce. Patrick hosted early meetings for the local chapter of the National Association for the Advancement

Marys Home for Aged Colored Women, 2823 Avenue K (modified). *Street Files Collection, courtesy of the Rosenberg Library (Galveston, TX).*

of Colored People (NAACP), first established in Galveston in 1918, at the house which later became the headquarters of the Mary Patrick Branch of the Young Women's Christian Association (YWCA) in the 1940s.

Another charitable organization that supported Galveston's Black community was the Albertine Yeager Day Nursery and Kindergarten. Albertine Hall Yeager (1897–1969) was born in Palestine, Texas, and dedicated fifty-two years of her life to the care and education of nearly one thousand Galveston youths. She always knew she wanted to work with children, as she had family members who operated childcare facilities. After she moved to Galveston to marry her high school sweetheart, Charles Yeager (1895–1985), the couple opened their first home daycare during World War I to provide working mothers a safe place where their children were taken care of for the daily rate of one dollar. With their center originally located at 3616 Avenue N, the Yeagers soon had 6 children under their care, all of whom had lost their fathers during World War I. In 1918, Mama Yeager, as she was known, was left to run the operation alone after Charles was inducted into the military. Upon his return in 1919, he found employment as a longshoreman on Galveston's wharf and worked a second job at the Armour Meat Packing Company to help support their growing nursery and daycare. As their clientele grew, the Yeagers eventually moved to 1111 32nd Street. They continued to finance their enterprise through admission fees subsidized by Mr. Yeager's salaries, even as enrollment increased to a daily attendance of 108 children by 1931. Their facility accepted children from infancy and would keep them until they were teenagers, and it served a diverse population, accommodating working parents, providing after-school care and taking in neglected children and orphans (who lived with the Yeagers).

Albertine Hall Yeager. *Name Files Photograph Collection, courtesy of the Rosenberg Library (Galveston, TX).*

On January 3, 1932, the *Galveston Daily News* posted an article under the headline "Appeal Made for Aid for Negro Day Nursery Here." The article stated that funds from the Community Chest (United Way) had been allocated and that donations were welcome. As a result of the article, individuals and business owners donated enough money over the years for the Yeagers to continue their mission. In 1934, during the annual Community Chest donation campaign on Galveston's local radio station KLUF, Mama Yeager spoke about the daycare, which was then known as the Albertine Yeager Day Nursery. Other groups that participated in the donation drive included the Negro Women's Hospital Aid and Marys Home for Aged Negro Women.

In 1969, shortly before her death, Mama Yeager received $60,000 in grants from the Kempner and Moody Foundations that provided assurance her work would be perpetuated. In 1975, a ribbon-cutting ceremony for new facilities was held, and in 1988, Albertine Yeager's Home for Children merged with the Galveston's Children's Home, the Lasker Home for Orphaned Children and the YWCA of Galveston to become the Children's Center Incorporated. With a combined history that spans nearly 145 years, the center continues the Yeagers' mission to provide protection, housing and counseling for Galveston County children and families.

Other organizations that formed during the Jim Crow era to assist Galveston's African American community included the local chapter of the National Council of Negro Women. Formed in 1946, the organization advocated for the use of collective power focused on issues that concerned Black women, families and communities. The Willing Workers Club, formed in 1923 by a group of African American ladies from local churches, supplied assistance to Black families at various levels. Men's groups, such as the Adelphi Club, Top Hatters, Diplomats and Sportsmen's Social Charity Club, formed during the same time period with the same mission: to serve Galveston's African American community wherever needed. In addition, the local chapters of several national African American sororities and fraternal organizations provided aid to families in need and offered vocational guidance conferences, organized educational symposiums, health fairs and school vaccination campaigns. They also facilitated voter registration drives and recognized outstanding African American students with college scholarships.

EDUCATIONAL EQUALITY

Education has always been considered the gateway to becoming a productive citizen by many African Americans. Even during slavery, reading and writing were the skills sought for survival and to understand the environment in which they lived. Those who could read and write secretly taught others. In 1869, the Barnes Institute, a freemen's school, became the first school established in Galveston for African Americans. Around 1881, state funds became available specifically for African American education and the construction of two primary schools, Galveston's East District and West District. Central High School, founded in 1885, was Texas's first African American high school and remained the only high school in the state for African Americans for several years. Students commuted to Galveston from surrounding cities to earn a high school diploma; for those who found the commute difficult, their parents rented rooms in homes near the school's campus. As the esteemed reputation of Galveston's Black campuses grew, many Black educators were dedicated to the betterment of the education experience for both students and faculty and support staff.

HISTORIC SIDEBAR
JESSIE MCGUIRE DENT, JOHN CLOUSER
AND DR. LEON MORGAN

Jessie May McGuire Dent (1892–1948) was an active member of the Colored Teachers State Association of Texas and was involved when the Texas Commission on Democracy in Education formed to promote racial equality for African American schools and advocate for better opportunities for African American educators through equal pay and access to administrative positions. McGuire was born in Galveston, and after she graduated as valedictorian from Central High School in 1909, she attended Howard University in Washington, D.C., where she was one of the twenty-two founding members of Delta Sigma Theta sorority, which was organized on Howard's campus on January 13, 1913. A few weeks after the sorority was formed, the group of women marched in the women's suffrage parade in Washington, D.C. After she completed her studies at Howard, McGuire returned to Galveston in 1913 and taught at Central High School, where she later became the dean of girls.

Back in her hometown, McGuire continued her sorority's mission to be active in one's community. She was part of the congregation of Avenue L Baptist Church, lent her voice to civic issues, supported the local suffrage movement and took a leadership role to assist the underserved through memberships in the Negro Divisions of the American Red Cross and Galveston's Community Chest, a forerunner to the United Way. In 1924, she married attorney Thomas Henry Dent, and the following year, she was elected to the first executive committee for the newly formed Colored Independent Voters League for Galveston County. In 1941, she established a Galveston chapter of Delta Sigma Theta sorority.

In 1943, Jessie McGuire Dent sued the board of trustees for the public free schools of the City of Galveston and demanded equal pay for African American teachers, deans, secretaries and principals. The suit was filed by the state's leading African American attorney for the NAACP, William J. Durham of Sherman, Texas. The judgment, issued in Galveston, Texas, on June 15, 1943, by United States judge T.M. Kennerly, ruled in favor of the plaintiff and instructed the Galveston school district to equalize pay for African American teachers, deans, secretaries and principals over a period of three years.

McGuire Dent's court fight to equalize pay for Black individuals employed by the Galveston school district was spearheaded by John Henry Clouser (1899–1987). Born in Velasco, Texas, and a graduate of Galveston's Central High

Jessie McGuire Dent.
Courtesy of Old Central Cultural Center Inc.

John Clouser. *Private collection, courtesy of the John Clouser family.*

School class of 1918, Clouser was a noted educator, NAACP official, civil rights activist and religious leader. His teaching career spanned over forty-eight years, during which he advocated for social justice reforms, teachers' rights and the desegregation of schools. In the classroom, Clouser incorporated safety patrols into physical education classes, taught students the basics of banking and organized scout troops for African American youth. He developed health and hygiene classes and took students to UTMB (the University of Texas Medical Branch at Galveston) to witness firsthand the ravages to the human body caused by tuberculosis, syphilis and other infectious microbes, and he accompanied students to the police station to view jail cells and attend lectures given by officers on venereal diseases. Clouser's objective on these seemingly unorthodox trips was to increase awareness and thereby discourage the spread of disease and bad behavior. His lessons tied in with the United States Public Health Service Program, which awarded the local program national recognition. With this spotlight, Clouser became chairman of National Negro Health Week, an annual event celebrated every April. The event began at church on Sunday, where sermons were planned around health and hygiene, and ended the following Saturday with a parade, picnic and games.

In 1946, Clouser became state treasurer for the NAACP. As a member of the executive committee, he worked closely with Supreme Court Justice Thurgood Marshall and was instrumental in filing numerous lawsuits involving the segregation of public schools and public housing for Black people in Galveston and across the state. Clouser was involved in the fights to allow Herman Sweat to enter the University of Texas Law School and Herman Barnett to enter the University of Texas Medical Branch. Clouser also mentored Kelton Sams, who would become instrumental in Galveston's civil rights movement, and urged him to lead the youth chapter

Dedication
Former Principals of Central High School

J. R. GIBSON
1886-1936

W. J. MASON
1936-1941

DR. L. A. MORGAN
1941-1967

The three principals of Central High School, including Dr. Leon Morgan, the last principal to serve the campus. Morgan held the position from 1941 to 1967. *Courtesy of Old Central Cultural Center Inc.*

of the NAACP. As a forerunner of the civil rights movement and advocate for social justice reforms, Clouser's involvement and willingness to fight for what he believed in left a legacy of change that is appreciated by all races today.

Another outstanding educator who dedicated their career to the betterment of Galveston's school system was Dr. Leon Augustus Morgan (1909–1993). Born in Houston, Texas, Morgan attended Paul Quinn College in Dallas before he

85

transferred to Wiley College in Marshall, where he earned his bachelor's degree in 1932. In 1933, Morgan was hired to teach English at Central High School. In addition to his classroom duties, Morgan coached Central's basketball and debate teams and edited the school's newspaper. He was soon promoted and served as principal for two elementary campuses before he returned to Central's campus as principal in 1941. During his tenure, Morgan wrote the school's alma mater, "Central High," and initiated the publication of the first yearbook in 1945–46. In 1942, Morgan chose former teacher Virginia Gloria Banks to provide the commencement speech at Central's graduation ceremony. Banks was the wife of Willette Banks, the principal of Prairie View State College, and was the first woman ever selected to address Central High School's graduating seniors.

The author of numerous published articles that include "Student Participation in School Control," "Follow-Up Studies on Discipline," "Negro Business in Galveston," "Experiment in Continuous Evaluation" and "The Science and Mathematics Programs in Texas," Morgan earned his doctorate degree from the University of Texas in 1956. Actively involved in the community, Morgan was the first African American to serve on several committees and boards, including the Galveston City Council Committee for Human Rights and the Galveston Civil Service Commission, where he remained twenty years. As chairperson of the Citizens Advisory Committee on Desegregation of Galveston Public Schools, Morgan assisted the school district when the city's two high schools, the all-White Ball High and Central High, merged in 1968. In addition, Morgan taught classes at Prairie View A&M University, Texas Southern University in Houston and Texas College in Tyler, Texas. After more than forty years with the Galveston school district, Morgan retired in 1974. In a 1969 interview, he was asked: "Who was the most famous student you've ever taught?" To which he replied, "Why, they were all famous, at least they were to me." In 1977, the Galveston Independent School Board renamed Carver Elementary School on Avenue N between 35th and 37th Streets L.A. Morgan Elementary School to honor Morgan's legacy of unwavering dedication to the students, school district and community.

MEDICAL TRAILBLAZERS

Where laws and society's customs dictated behavior, physicians in the Jim Crow South faced obstacles, indignities and dangers. If a Black physician was asked to come to the home of a White patient or call on a patient in a White hospital, they entered through the back door. Separate waiting rooms were common when doctors of either race treated both Black and White patients.

The Medical Department of the University of Texas at Galveston built the first hospital for African Americans in 1902. The building was paid for through a $15,000 anonymous donation from a New York philanthropist and $35,000 from the 1900 Storm Central Relief Committee.

After World War I, the growth of the city of Galveston placed a strain on the capacity of the existing hospital, and a second hospital for African Americans was opened on August 31, 1937.

Groundbreaking pioneers who provided for the medical needs of Black Galvestonians during the Jim Crow era included Dr. Joseph Mack Mosely Sr. (1899–1946), a graduate of Meharry Medical College in Nashville, Tennessee, known as the first medical college to admit African Americans. Mosely opened his first medical practice in Galveston in 1916, and his son, Dr. Joseph Mack Mosely II, would later join his father's firm. Other

Galveston's first hospital for African Americans, built in 1902. *Courtesy of Truman G. Blocker Jr., History of Medicine Collections, Moody Medical Library, UTMB (Galveston, TX).*

A second hospital for African Americans opened on August 31, 1937. *Courtesy of Truman G. Blocker Jr., History of Medicine Collections, Moody Medical Library, UTMB (Galveston, TX).*

standouts in the medical field include the Stanton family, community activists who counted five medical professionals among them; Herman Barnett, the first African American student admitted to the University of Texas Medical School at Galveston (UTMB); and Wilina Gatson, the University of Texas Medical Branch's first African American to graduate from the school of nursing.

HISTORIC SIDEBAR
LEADERS IN MEDICINE

Dr. Mary Susan Smith Moore (1865–1965) was the first Black woman physician to practice medicine in Texas. After she graduated from Meharry Medical College in 1898, she and her husband, James D. Moore, established the forty-bed Hubbard

Sanitarium in Galveston in 1903, which provided care for Black patients into the mid-1920s. Joseph Mack Mosely, MD (1899–1946), was born in Texarkana, Texas, and after he graduated from Meharry in 1913, he opened a medical practice in Galveston in 1916. He is listed in the 1924–25 *Galveston City Directory* as a physician and surgeon who specialized in "diseases of women." His office was located in the Oleander Hotel building at 421½ 25th Street. His son and namesake, Joseph Mack Moseley II, MD (1921–1960), was also born on Galveston Island. He attended Fisk University in Nashville, Tennessee, and graduated in 1941, after which he enrolled at Meharry Medical College. After he graduated from Meharry in 1944, he interned at the Homer C. Phillips Hospital in St. Louis, Missouri, and later at St. Mary's Infirmary in Galveston. Dr. Mosely II was active in the community and served on the board of the Volunteer Health League. With a specialty in internal medicine, he soon joined his father's medical practice at the Oleander Hotel building, where the Drs. Stanton were also located.

Rufus Stanton Sr. (1885–1955) was the eldest of four brothers, all of whom entered the medical field. Born in Crockett, Texas, Stanton worked as a barber and, later, a pharmacist before he became a dentist. To pay his way through Meharry Medical College in Nashville, Tennessee, Stanton worked as a Pullman porter on the railroads. After he graduated, Stanton moved to Galveston and opened a dental practice in 1915. His brother Robert (1891–1961) attended Meharry Medical College and moved to Galveston after he graduated. At their medical practice, Stanton and Stanton at 501 25th Street, Robert practiced medicine the old-fashioned way, making house calls and delivering babies in the homes of his patients. He spoke Spanish fluently and delivered most of the Hispanic babies in Galveston during that time. He mixed a lot of his own medicines and dispensed them to his patients as needed.

The third brother, Reapher Stanton (1893–1973), graduated from Meharry Medical College School of Pharmacy and returned to the island to work at the Island City Drug Store at 2728 Postoffice Street. Owned and operated by his father, Sandy Hezekiah Stanton, the store was located on the northeast corner of Postoffice and 28th Streets and catered to the African American community. The business closed during the Great Depression, but Reapher continued to work as an independent pharmacist until his retirement. The youngest brother, Elbert (1900–1964), attended both Wiley College in Marshall Texas and Meharry Medical College. After he graduated from Meharry in the 1930s, he returned to Galveston and joined his brothers in their medical practice. During his career, he served as the physician for the Galveston's "Negro" schools and was active in politics, running for various political offices on multiple occasions.

Rufus "Billy" Stanton Jr. (1925–2004) graduated from Wiley College and received his doctorate of dentist science from Meharry Medical College. In 1953, he joined his uncles Drs. Elbert and Robert Stanton in their practice before he opened his own office. He practiced dentistry for over forty years and also served on the United States Bank's board of directors, the city charter review board and the board of directors at St. Vincent's House, a charitable organization that serves the disadvantaged and poor of Galveston County.

Herman Aladdin Barnett (1926–1973) broke the color barrier in 1949, when he became the first African American admitted to the University of Texas Medical School in Galveston and, later, the first African American Texan to graduate from a Texas medical college licensed to practice medicine in the state. Born in Austin, Texas, Barnett graduated with honors from the University of Texas Medical School in 1953. He completed his residency in surgery in 1958 and specialized in trauma, focused on how the body changed when it experienced emergencies and during postoperative recoveries. In 1968, Barnett completed his second residency at St. Joseph's Hospital in Houston. During his lifetime, he was affiliated with numerous hospitals, including the University of Texas Medical Branch (UTMB) Galveston hospitals, the Galveston County Memorial Hospital and Hermann Hospital in Houston. After Barnett was killed in a plane crash, his friends and colleagues established the Herman A. Barnett Award, which has been given annually to outstanding UTMB medical students since 1974. In 1978, Dr. Barnett posthumously received the Ashbel

Smith Award, the University of Texas Medical Branch at Galveston's highest honor.

Wilina Garner Mitchell Gatson (1925–2011) was the first African American woman to graduate from the University of Texas Medical Branch Bachelor of Science Nursing Program and is recognized as a "Distinguished Alumnus" in the University of Texas Medical Branch Hall of Fame. Gatson graduated from Galveston's Central High School with honors and was a lifelong resident of Galveston who was active in the religious, civic and community affairs of the city. Her drive to achieve and excel, despite the racial, gender and cultural limitations of that time, led her to become a trailblazer in her field. In addition to being recognized as the first Black graduate of UTMB School of Nursing BS program, she was named Outstanding UTMB School of Nursing Student of the Year in 1958 and was an officer of the UTMBSN Alumni Association. During her career, Gatson served as the director of nursing at the Moody State School for Cerebral Palsied Children and the nursing house supervisor at Galveston's St. Mary's Hospital.

While making inroads on an individual level, Gatson continually fought for all people through her work with the Civil Liberty League; the NAACP, where she was chairperson of the Legal Redress Committee; and organizations that included the Versatile Dames Society, the Sickle Cell Foundation, the Galveston Chapter of Jack and Jill of America and the Black Nurses' Association. In addition to serving as a former president of American Legion Auxiliary Gus Allen III Unit 614, Gatson organized the first junior auxiliary in Galveston, from which came the first Black color guard in the state of Texas. Gatson was president of Delta Sigma Theta sorority's Galveston chapter and active on committees associated with the American Baptist Eastern General Association of Texas Inc. and the American Baptist General Convention of Texas. Her biography has been featured in multiple publications, including *Personalities of the South, International Dictionary of Autobiographies, Who's Who Among Black Americans, Worlds Who's Who of Women* and *Who's Who of World's Intellectuals.*

BLACK TOURISM

During the Jim Crow era, Black Americans often faced difficulty and hardships when traveling. Even though discrimination was deemed illegal with the Civil Rights Act of 1875, some cities and states found ways to perpetuate discrimination against Black travelers. To avoid such racial prejudice, Black travelers relied on *The Negro Motorist Green-Book* to locate motels and restaurants that were welcoming to African Americans. Published from 1936 to 1967, the guidebooks were compiled and published by Victor Hugo Green, a Black postal worker from New York City who printed approximately fifteen thousand copies of his *Green-Book* annually.

Galveston businesses that welcomed Black patrons were included for the first time in the 1936 *Green-Book*. Lodging entries included a hotel, the Oleander, located at 421½ 25th Street (extant), and two tourist homes, Miss Georgia H. Freeman's house at 1414 29th Street and Mrs. Joseph Pope's (Teola) residence at 2824 Avenue M. The 1939 entry for Galveston also included John N. Rose's Gulf View Tavern at 28th Street and Seawall Boulevard, where segregation laws restricted African Americans' only access to the Gulf of Mexico to a one-block area sometimes called Brown Beach. Although entries for Galveston fluctuated over the years and grew to include the tourist-oriented enterprises of local businessmen Gus Allen and Thomas "T.D." Armstrong. The Oleander Hotel and Pope and Freeman's tourist homes were consistent *Green-Book* entries until 1964, when Galveston's businesses were included for the last time.

HISTORIC SIDEBAR
EARLY LEADERS IN TOURISM AND HOSPITALITY: ROBERT McGUIRE, GUS ALLEN, T.D. ARMSTRONG AND COURTNEY MURRAY

Within the boundaries of Brown Beach, policeman, businessman and civic activist Robert McGuire (1868–1920) established a beach resort in 1910 for Black patrons called McGuire Park. McGuire was born in Galveston to parents John and Fannie McGuire, who were themselves born into slavery in Georgia and Virginia, respectively. Robert McGuire's first notation in the *Galveston City Directory* came in 1884, when he was recorded as an employee in the Tremont Hotel's billiard room. By 1886, he was working alongside his father in Galveston's cotton sheds.

In 1890, McGuire married Alberta Mabson, and the couple moved to the corner of Avenue R and 28th Street on lots they purchased in 1893. In 1909, McGuire retired from the police department, and in 1910, he formed a partnership with William Lewis and Peter Antone to establish McGuire Park on his beachfront property. The park catered to Black patrons and included a two-story frame pavilion with a cupola that served as both a bathhouse and dance hall with two smaller buildings that housed a café and a club. The park became a popular destination for the Black community and was the site of church picnics, community fairs and Juneteenth celebrations.

In 1914, the City of Galveston condemned the buildings at McGuire Park, and a year later, it acquired all of McGuire's land along Avenue R between 27th and 28th Streets, which also included his home. In January 1915, the *City Times* reported:

> *McGuire Park, at Twenty-Eighth Avenue [sic] and Avenue R, will be sold to the City of Galveston, also Mr. McGuire's residence property, and Mrs. Richards', Miss L.P. Williams' and Messrs. T.P. Pope's and Robt. Davis'. These being colored citizens owning in a block that the Galveston park site is to cover as selected by the Galveston Commercial Association. The total amount to be paid these citizens is $18,500, as follows: Mr. McGuire, $11,500; Miss L.P. Williams, $2,500; Mrs. Richards, $1,000; Mr. Robert Davis, $2,000; Mr. T.P. Pope, $1,500. The McGuire Park was a resort for colored people, also the Pope property next to it. The earnest money has been paid to them all and it will not be long before they will receive the balance. Mr. Hoskins Foster represents Galveston's interest.*

After the city acquired his property, McGuire relocated his family home one block west, to 2818 Avenue R. McGuire Park was later renamed Menard Park, and in 1999, in response to a community petition, the Galveston Parks and Recreation Board and Galveston City Council voted to name the recreation center McGuire-Dent in honor of Robert McGuire and his

The McGuire-Dent Recreation Center (2222 28th Street) is located on the previous site of McGuire Park, an early beach resort for African Americans. *Courtesy of the Galveston Historical Foundation.*

daughter, educator and activist Jessie McGuire Dent.

In 1922, Augustus "Gus" Allen arrived in Galveston and soon established several tourist-oriented businesses along the segregated 2800 block of Seawall Boulevard focused on creating a welcoming atmosphere for African Americans. Born in Leesville, Louisiana, Allen's enterprises on Seawall Boulevard helped define Black life in Galveston. Within one block, Allen's enterprises included Gus Allen's Café, the Jambalaya Restaurant and Gus Allen's Villa Hotel. Although activities were limited to the area, many great memories were formed by visitors from all over the country. Allen also operated the Dreamland Café at 2704 Church Street and played a significant role in the success of other Black restauranteurs, including Nelson "Honey" Brown, who operated a very successful barbecue café, and Albert Fease, who leased space from Allen for a restaurant along the 2800 block of Seawall Boulevard.

Louisiana native Thomas D. Armstrong was a teacher in Port Arthur before he moved to Galveston in 1938 and became one of the most successful Black businessmen of the

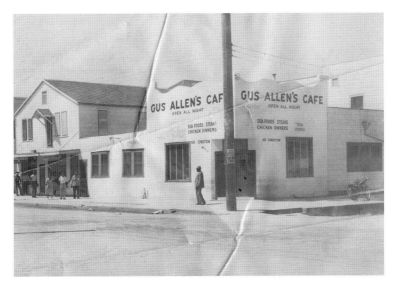

Gus Allen's Café, one of several establishments within the 2800 block of Seawall Boulevard that catered to Black patrons during the Jim Crow era. *G-Files: Hotels, Courtesy of the Rosenberg Library (Galveston, TX).*

Gus Allen's Hotel, also located within the one-block area of Galveston's segregated beachfront. *G-Files: Hotels, Courtesy of Rosenberg Library (Galveston, TX).*

Delegates T.D. Armstrong (*middle*) and Mack Hanna (*left*) depart Galveston in 1948, headed to the Texas Democratic Convention. *SC60_FF2, courtesy of the Rosenberg Library (Galveston, TX).*

time. With multiple investments in companies that catered to both Black tourists and local residents, Armstrong's business accomplishments included the Little Shamrock Motel and Coffee Shop, the Armstrong Drug Store, the BA&P Realty Company, T.D. Armstrong Realty, T.D.A. Investment Company, Armstrong-Strode Funeral Home and the Tyler Life Insurance Company, which became one of the largest Texas-owned, predominantly Black insurance companies in the state.

In 1948, Armstrong and Mack Hannah Jr., a Port Arthur businessman, became the first Black delegates from Texas to attend the Democratic Party National Convention. In 1961, Armstrong was the first African American elected to Galveston's City Council and was a delegate to the Democratic Party National Convention in 1964 and 1968. Armstrong's personal wealth was noted in printed articles published in *Ebony* magazine in September 1961, including a story titled "Negro Politician Makes Good in Texas: Plantation-Born Ex-Teacher Rises to Wealth and Post on Galveston City Council," followed by an article in the May 1962 issue of *Ebony* that declared Armstrong one of "America's 100 Richest Negroes." The list also included Harry Belafonte, Nat King Cole, Johnny

Mathis and Floyd Patterson.

During the 1940s, 1950s and 1960s, local businessman Courtney Murray (1902–2001) boosted the entertainment level for tourists and local residents through his promotional efforts that brought the top Black talent to Galveston's City Auditorium. Born in Grand Cane, Louisiana, Murray's promotions included appearances by Louis Jordan, Billy Eckstein, Sara Vaughn, Joe Turner, Peg Leg Bates, Bill "Bojangles" Robinson, Count Basie, Cab Calloway and His Cotton Club Orchestra, Lionel Hampton and His Orchestra, Charles Brown, Earl "Father" Hines, *Green-Book* founder Victor Hugo Green, Roy Milton and His Soul Senders, Duke Ellington, Nat King Cole and the International All Girl Orchestra and the Sweethearts of Rhythm—just to name a few.

Tickets were sold at Murray's Tip Top Café at 2627 Church Street, the City Auditorium and a few other select businesses. All of his advertisements included the statement "Section Reserved for Whites." On November 23, 1988, Texas governor William P. Clements Jr. presented Murray with a humanitarian award for his accomplishments, general contributions to the community and support of the military. The award cited his work in the Job Corp program and recognized his contributions during World War II.

Pioneer Performers, Artists and Atheletes

Galveston's Black community, like most others in Texas and the South, produced successful performers, artists and leaders for generations. Through activities in churches, schools and historically Black colleges and universities, young men and women developed skills and connections that became the foundations for their artistic endeavors. Many faced barriers or prohibition in certain, mostly White, venues and in the hospitality and entertainment sites that invited them. Some hotels, restaurants and nightclubs prohibited African Americans through segregation laws. Artists sometimes accepted their fate, but others canceled performances or relocated to open communities and venues. Through this process, a number of men and women were able to break through the color barrier and develop successful careers on their own to accomplish lifelong goals in music, art, sports and other areas appreciated today.

Despite the efforts of artists and their agents, many talented men and women (and groups) were booked around the country in popular venues and emerging centers of artistic talent. For others, including individuals facing dire economic opportunity in their home communities and states, migrating to the North or West offered their only real path to earn decent wages and meet career aspirations. The Great Migration, now documented by a number of historians, occurred between approximately 1910 and 1970. African Americans, motivated by the limitations to employment and access in social environments supported by Jim Crow laws and their enforcement, moved to major cities like Chicago, New York and Los Angeles. The migration separated families but introduced them to new jobs and careers and offered some economic independence. In many cases, they maintained their ties to their former hometowns. Galvestonians who moved to the Los Angeles area in the mid-twentieth century organized Old Central High School gatherings for former classmates and celebrated traditions like Juneteenth with family and friends. Many of these displaced "communities" still meet to renew and continue familiar Galveston traditions.

HISTORIC SIDEBAR
NOTABLE ARTISTS AND ATHLETES: MAUD CUNEY HARE, JACK JOHNSON AND OTHERS

Musician, writer and activist Maud Cuney Hare (1874–1936) was born in Galveston to mixed-race parents Norris Wright Cuney and Adelina Dowdy. Her musical influence began at home, where her father played the violin and her mother played the piano and sang. After Maud graduated from Central High School in 1890, she enrolled at the New England Conservatory of Music in Boston, Massachusetts, to study piano. While she was at the conservatory, a group of White students pressured school administrators to bar Maud, as well as another Black student, from campus accommodations. After she consulted her father, Maud informed school administrators that she refused to move. Her father also refused to move her and criticized the school for dishonoring "the noble men and women abolitionists of Massachusetts who had fought against prejudice." Maud later wrote in her book *Norris Wright Cuney: A Tribune of the Black People* that she "insisted upon proper treatment."

When she graduated from the conservatory, Maud returned to Texas and began private studies with pianist Emil Ludwig in Austin while she also taught at the Texas Deaf and Blind Institute for Colored Youths and performed publicly. At one of her performances at the

Musician and writer Maud Cuney Hare in January 1913. *Public domain.*

Austin Opera House, management demanded Black audience members be segregated and seated in the balcony. Maud canceled the show and performed instead before an integrated audience at the Texas Institute for Colored Youths. Maud moved to Chicago after her parents died and married Dr. J. Frank McKinley, also of mixed race, who demanded she identify as Spanish American like he did. Raised to embrace her Black heritage, she found the demand unacceptable, yet when her daughter was born in 1900, Maud was noted as Spanish American on the child's birth certificate. Maud eventually took her daughter and moved to Texas for a teaching position at Prairie View Agricultural and Mechanical College. McKinley filed for divorce and received custody of the little girl. Maud returned to Boston to be closer to her child and eventually married William Parker Hare in 1904.

After Maude married Hare, she founded the Musical Art Studio to promote concerts and a little theater movement in the Black community. She toured throughout the eastern United States, performing public recitals and lectures until 1913, when she began collaborations with William Howard Richardson, a Canadian baritone singer. They toured together for twenty years, often stopping in Galveston, where they performed at the Wesley Tabernacle Methodist Episcopal Church and the Lincoln Theatre on 25th Street. Back in Boston, Maud founded the Allied Arts Centre in 1927, the first arts center for

African Americans. In addition to her musical and theatrical accomplishments, her literary works include *Creole Songs* (1921), her poetry collection *The Message of the Trees* (1918), the play *Antar of Araby* (1929) about an Arabian poet and *Negro Musicians and Their Music* (1936), which documents the development of African American music.

Politically, Maud was among the first women to join the Niagara Movement in 1907, a Black civil rights organization founded in 1905 by W.E.B. Du Bois and William Monroe Trotte. In 1909, the organization became known as the National Association for the Advancement of Colored People (NAACP), and Maud often wrote articles for *Crisis*, the NAACP magazine. Maud and Du Bois were engaged to be married, but by mutual agreement, the couple broke the engagement. They remained good friends throughout their lifetimes, and after her death Du Bois wrote:

> *Maud Cuney was the bravest woman I have ever known. For those born in adversity, fighting fate becomes a habit, rather than virtue; but when one is born to the purple and is first in mid-life overwhelmed by successive and relentless blows of every kind of cruelty and adversity, then to keep one's chin up, the eye unflinching, and the courage unfaltering, calls for the sort of soul men seldom see.*

Frederick Charles Tillis, PhD. *Courtesy of Old Central Cultural Center Inc.*

Frederick Charles Tillis (1930–2020) was another Galveston-born author and composer who was exposed to music at a young age, courtesy of his musical mother. In elementary school, he joined the drum and bugle corps band, performed with a jazz band when he was twelve years old and played saxophone in the band at Central High School. In 1946, Tillis enrolled in Wiley College on a music scholarship and was hired as the college's band director after he graduated. He remained in that position until he entered the University of Iowa's school for graduate music program. He suspended his studies during the

Korean War to join the United States Air Force and became the first Black band director of the 356th Air Force Band. He later returned to his graduate studies at North Texas College in Denton, Texas. After graduation, Tillis returned to the University of Iowa to finish his PhD. Upon its completion in 1963, he taught at several colleges and universities. In his later life, Tillis authored multiple books of poetry, which were published between 1989 and 2006.

Award-winning music teacher and past trustee for Galveston ISD Izola Fedford Collins (1929–2017) was a Galveston native and well known as a historian, author, musician, choral director and composer. After she graduated from Central High School at the age of fourteen, she enrolled in Prairie View State College and majored in music education. By the second semester of 1943, during World War II, all of Prairie View's traveling all-male band, the Collegiates, had been drafted. In response, Prairie View's Co-ed All-Girl Band organized and sought women to replace the men. Collins soon joined and played trumpet as the co-eds performed the same music as the male band. Prairie View's Co-ed All-Girl Band traveled on the weekends, and during the summer months, members were paid for their appearances and had a booking agent by the spring of 1944. Always well dressed, the co-eds performed in Houston and on military bases, especially for Black soldiers, who were often overlooked. Their appearances included performances for the Tuskegee Airmen and concerts at Black colleges and Black theaters, including New York's Apollo Theater and other venues throughout the South, where they experienced harassment as they searched for restaurants, gas stations, hotels or rooming houses while on the road. When they performed in New York, the band stayed at the Cecil Hotel in Harlem, near the Apollo Theater, and received great coverage in the Black press with nothing reported in White newspapers.

After Collins earned a bachelor's degree from Prairie View and master's degree from Northwestern University in Evanston, Illinois, she taught music and choir at the elementary and high school level before she became the band director at Hitchcock High School in Hitchcock, Texas. A few years after she retired from teaching, the Galveston Historical Foundation presented

Barry Eugene Carter White was born on the island. His family relocated to California when he was an infant. *Courtesy of Old Central Cultural Center Inc.*

a seminar titled "Women's Roles in World War II" that featured Collins and her trumpet. The audience went wild, clapping and foot stomping, with yells of encouragement that Collins "still had it."

Perhaps the best-known singer-songwriter, recorder, producer, arranger and musician with ties to the island is Barry White (1944–2003). Born Barry Eugene Carter, his family moved to California while he was an infant. Introduced to music by his mother's collection of classical records, he would rise to success during the 1960s with *Billboard* hits that charted at the platinum, gold and silver levels. While White was raised in California, other entertainers born on the island and raised in Galveston eventually migrated to the West Coast in search of better opportunities. In the early 1940s, Camille Agnes Browning (1914–1993) headed to the West Coast and joined the Roy Milton Trio under the stage name Camille Howard. Together, they recorded and released the instrumental tune "Camille's Boogie" and "When I Grow Too Old to Dream," which featured Howard on vocals. In 1948, her first solo record was released and was an immediate hit that sold more than one hundred thousand copies. Tony Russell "Charles" Brown (1922–1999) was born in Texas City, Texas, and graduated from Central High School when it was the only high school in Galveston County for African Americans. He relocated to Los Angeles, California, in 1943, and there, he met musician Jonny Moore, who offered Brown a job with his band the Three Blazers. They recorded the hit "Driftin Blues," featuring Brown on lead vocals. Brown recorded several more hits with

Singer, songwriter, composer, arranger and playwright Eddie Curtis. *Courtesy of Bernard Curtis.*

Moore, including his best known song, "Merry Christmas Baby," which was recorded in 1947.

Singer, songwriter, composer, arranger and playwright Eddie Curtis (1927–1983) was a versatile instrumentalist educated at the Boston Conservatory of Music, the Berklee School of Music and the University of California at Los Angeles. Curtis composed hundreds of songs for other artists, including Ray Charles, Connie Francis and Steve Miller. Blues and jazz singer Esther Mae Jones (1935–1984) performed under the name Little Esther Phillips during the 1950s and early 1960s. She moved to California when she was a teenager, and after she arrived, bluesman Johnny Otis approached her and added her to his roster of performers. Two of her greatest hits were "Mistrustin' Blues" and a remake of Dinah Washington's "What a Difference a Day Makes." After trumpeter Richard Gene Williams (1931–1985) completed the music studies program at Wiley College, he broke the mold and headed to New York City, where he enrolled at the Manhattan School of Music. After he completed his graduate studies, Williams remained in New York and led bands under his own name, performed with Broadway orchestras and was featured by many big-name bands, including Duke Ellington's. His 1960 recording "New Horn in Town" was the only recording under his name.

Black photographer Lucius William Harper (1867–1920) was listed in the *Galveston City Directory* numerous times and was associated with various occupations in addition to photography, including house mover, scroll sawyer and artist. Born in Sabine Pass, Texas, he was married twice and had three children with his second wife, Rachel Love. From 1893 to 1914, Harper resided at 2897 Avenue M½, where he also operated a photography studio. Between 1910 and 1913, Harper operated a second photography studio for African Americans in Dallas, Texas, at 1716 Allen Street.

Harper utilized a gelatin silver process for his photographs, a common method that produced black and white photographs during the 1890s. His work included several distinctive photographs, yet few exist today. One notable photograph that does survive in the collection of the Smithsonian National Museum of African American History and Culture is titled *Off for School.* The black and white oval photograph depicts his son, Lucius Harper Jr., in a suit with short pants holding his schoolbooks slung over his shoulder. In 1914, the *Galveston City Directory* listed Lucius Harper Jr. working as a photographer with his father. After Harper Sr. died, Harper Jr. partnered with Mathew Lilly and established Lilly and Harper Studios at 421½ 25th Street in the Oleander Hotel, and in 1924, he opened Harper's Studio at 1303 29th Street.

After Lucius Harper arrived in Galveston, another Black photographer named John Ellis Palmer (1891–1964) from Many, Louisiana, came to Galveston in 1916 and opened a

Off to School, photographed by Lucius Harper Sr. *Courtesy of the Collection of the Smithsonian, National Museum of African American History and Culture.*

photography studio at 2715½ Market Street. Most of Palmer's photographs were black and white gelatin silver prints, although a few were hand colored. Through the years, Palmer took thousands of portraits and candid photographs of Black Texans that captured the life of Galveston's Black community in the early and mid-twentieth century. During World War I, Palmer was a corporal in the U.S. Army. In 1930, he married Cleo Keys, and by 1932, he had moved his studio to the 2500 block of Market Street, where he advertised commercial and portrait photography and enlargements with "Kodak Finishing." Palmer resided in Galveston for the rest of his life. He was active in the Black community and served as president of the Texas State Lodge of Elks in 1944; he was also a member of the St. Lawrence Lodge 258 and received the thirty-third degree in the Holy Royal Arch Masons.

Veteran motion-picture actor Hayes E. Robertson (1893–1939) was born in Galveston and moved to California, where he became an actor and comedian for the Keystone Comedy Company. As with so many actors and entertainers with inconsistent work, Robertson also worked as a janitor at Los Angeles City Hall, but between 1915 and 1936, he appeared in more than thirty movies and was employed by several movie studios as a stand-in. Most of his performances were uncredited and included typical roles for African Americans during that period—cook, Native chief, train porter and conductor, butler, chauffeur and restaurant waiter. Other uncredited roles included appearances in the controversial *The Birth of a Nation* (1915) as a man who gets up and walks inside a building while members of the Ku Klux Klan watch, a postal carrier in *His Silent Racket* (1933) and a man at a funeral in *Imitation of Life* (1934). Robertson was credited for his performances in the movies *War Feathers* (1926), *Wild Beauty* (1927) and *Shameful Behavior* (1926). With regard to his role in *Shameful Behavior*, the *Los Angeles Evening Citizen* newspaper stated, "Hayes Robertson, well known colored comedian, is playing an important part in *Shameful Behavio*r," while the *Bakersfield Californian* commented, "The supporting cast consists of real troupers: Scott Seaton, Hayes Robertson, William Bailey and J. Gordon Russell."

The most famous athlete born in Galveston is arguably John Arthur "Jack" Johnson (1878–1946), the first Black Heavy Weight Champion of the World. Johnson dropped out of the Galveston school system around the sixth or seventh grade to work on Galveston's wharf, where he honed his fighting skills. His first debut as a professional occurred in Galveston on November 1, 1897. As he continued to fight and win, his colorful lifestyle did not sit well with many people, especially White people. In 1912, Johnson was arrested for violating the Mann Act, which prohibited "transporting women across state lines for immoral purposes." He skipped bail and left the United States before he eventually returned and served his sentence. While incarcerated, Johnson made improvements on a wrench and was issued a patent for his invention (U.S. patent no. 141121). After his release in 1921, Johnson continued to fight in boxing exhibitions well into his sixties.

Galveston native John Arthur "Jack" Johnson was the first African American heavyweight champion of the world. *Courtesy of the Library of Congress.*

In 1952, Ray Dohn Dillon (1929–2021) became the first African American from Galveston to enter the National Football League (NFL). Drafted by the Detroit Lions, Dillon returned to Galveston after a knee injury ended his professional football career and was hired by the City of Galveston as the recreation director for Norris Wright Cuney Recreational Center. In 1957, the Galveston Independent School District hired Dillon to teach swimming and coach football at Central High School. When the two public high schools merged in the 1968–69 school year, Dillon was named chief of the district's police department and appointed head of human relations and attendance. Charley Ferguson (1939–2023) was drafted by the NFL in 1961. Ferguson moved to Galveston with his family when he was young, and after he graduated from Central High School, he excelled on the football fields of Central and Tennessee State Universities. Ferguson played with the Cleveland Browns until 1962, when he was picked up by the Minnesota Vikings. A year later, Ferguson was traded to the Buffalo Bills of the American Football League (AFL) and participated in playoff games for four straight years, winning AFL Championships in 1964 and 1965. In 1965, Ferguson was named an AFL All-Star.

MOVEMENT TOWARD CIVIL RIGHTS

By the middle of the twentieth century, the pursuit of equal civil rights had become a focus for African Americans across the country. A primary goal of the effort was the desegregation of public accommodations, including transportation options, educational facilities and city services. In Texas, the state branch of the NAACP provided leadership and legal assistance for local campaigns and contributed to some notable successes during the 1950s. In Beaumont, a court order ended the segregation of public parks in 1954. Corpus Christi voluntarily desegregated its public pool two years later. While the informal segregation of Houston's public transportation system continued through the 1950s, the city at least stopped enforcing the rule after 1954.

In Galveston, civil rights efforts gained momentum in the 1940s and early 1950s. In addition to Jessie McGuire Dent's successful lawsuit in 1943 for equal pay for Black educators, administrators and custodians, in 1949, the University of Texas Medical Branch (UTMB) at Galveston admitted its first Black student, and in 1957, nearly one hundred years after the first Black men were named to the city's police force, the Galveston Fire Department hired its first Black firemen. The men were stationed at Star State Company No. 3 (2828 Market Street) and were included in a group of eight hose and laddermen, who were added to the Galveston Fire Department on Thursday, November 21, 1957, by the board of the city commissioners on the recommendation of police and fire commissioner Walter B. Rourke.

Informal links between Star State Company No. 3 and the Black community had developed by 1927. In that year, a close mayoral election pitted incumbent Jack E. Pearce against fire and police commissioner R.P. Williamson. Black voters favored Williamson and actively supported his candidacy. On April 8, a report surfaced that said, in a political maneuver, Pearce's allies had promised to "turn fire station No. 3, located at 29th and Market streets, over to the negroes, and that the entire personnel of this station would be made up of negroes." The announcement demonstrated the perception of links between Star State Company No. 3 and the Black community in 1927 and marked the first documented attempt to give Black Galvestonians a role within the municipal fire department. Pearce won the election but did not uphold the agreement with Star State Company No. 3, which continued to operate with exclusively White personnel. At least as early as 1941, the station was the polling location for the predominantly Black Precinct 6. The city also housed a driver's license office inside the building.

Finally, on November 2, 1957, the *Galveston Daily News* announced that the fire department hired Black firefighters for the first time in its history. Police and fire commissioner Walter B. Rourke Jr. explained that all eight men—five White and three Black—were to "serve as hose and laddermen at Star State Company No. 3, 29th and Market." As part of the preparations for the new personnel, the station added new accommodations. Three weeks after the announcement, the department added three African Americans: Lucious Pope, Leroy Small and Genoice Walker.

HISTORIC SIDEBAR
GALVESTON'S FIRST BLACK FIREMEN

Lucious Trust Pope (1938–2022) was born in Ringgold, Louisiana, but moved to Galveston in 1955, where he graduated from Central High School in 1957. In Pope's words:

> *I happened to be walking down the street somewhere on 29th near H, and I ran into a black police officer and I think I was inquiring of him if he knew where I could find a better job. And he said to me "Police Chief Rourke…made the campaign promise that if he won he would hire some black firemen," he says, "he won so why don't you go down and put in an application." And that I did. Little did I think I would pass it, but I did.*

Pope worked at Star State Company No. 3 for three years before he left Galveston to serve in the U.S. Army. After he was discharged in 1964, he returned to Galveston and the fire department. He remained there for one year before he moved to California. He later sold insurance and organized the Greater New Vision Missionary Baptist Church in Los Angeles, where he served as the congregation's pastor.

Genoice Laurice Walker (1939–2005) moved to Galveston from Grapeland, Texas, at the age of sixteen. During his fire department career, Walker became a training officer and captain at the No. 3. station. He designed the first fireman training field to train firemen in life support and rescue technologies

Added to the fire department in 1957, Genoice Walker, Lucious Pope and Leroy Small were Galveston's first Black firemen. *Courtesy of the City of Galveston Fire Department.*

and often assisted fire departments in other communities with personnel training. After he retired from the fire department, Walker continued to work in various jobs that included stints at the Galveston County Sheriff's Office.

Leroy Lawrence Small (1931–1995) was a Galveston native, Korean War veteran and the oldest of the three Black firemen appointed in 1957. Little is known about Small's life and his fire department career. By the 1980s, he had relocated to Berkley, California, but later moved to Portland, Oregon. In a 2017 interview, Lucious Pope remembered Small as a quiet man who tended to stick to himself.

At the time that Pope, Walker and Small began their fire department careers, shifts lasted twenty-four hours. When Pope arrived for his first day in late November 1957, he found that the White firefighters had prepared for their arrival with the construction of a separate kitchen and separate sleeping quarters. As Pope explained:

Much to my surprise, they showed me to the back of their kitchen they where they had built a new kitchen for me, or for us. And so, I had a separate kitchen. They had given me a refrigerator, a stove, dishes, everything. That was where I ate my meals—in "my kitchen," I called it. And upstairs there was a large section for the men to sleep. Many cots, many beds. And to my further surprise,

*they showed me my bedroom. They had built a new bedroom in the
back upstairs, where I was to sleep. There were three beds in there
I recall, one for each of us.*

In the original station configuration at Star State Company
No. 3, the Black firefighters responded to emergencies by
running through the White firemen's bedroom to slide down
the fireman's pole. Soon, fire department leaders built a second
pole in the back specifically for the Black firemen to use. Pope
remembered that, despite the separate accommodations, the
White and Black firemen got along well enough. The onus
was on Pope, Walker and Small to recognize and respect
boundaries. Their biggest source of frustration was the lack of
opportunities for career advancement.

By the time Pope returned to Galveston in 1964, after a
three-year stint in the army, he found that racial separations
inside the fire department had eased. Black and White firemen
had begun to eat together and to sleep in the same bedrooms.
The second pole at the station had been long since been
removed. During the early 1960s, the fire department hired
more Black firemen. Star State Company No. 3 continued to
provide protection service for the north side neighborhoods
through most of the 1960s.

AS RACIAL TENSIONS WITHIN GALVESTON's integrated fire department began
to ease, a civil rights protest in February 1960 led by students in Greensboro,
North Carolina, began to awaken similar tensions in segregated communities
all over the country. Organized as nonviolent yet determined, the sit-in at
Greensboro's Woolworth lunch counter involved four students from North
Carolina Agricultural and Technical State University who politely refused
to leave the White-only lunch counter when asked. No arrests were made,
and the students remained seated until the store closed. The next day,
over a dozen more students joined the peaceful protest, which attracted
the attention of the local media. On the third day, the Student Executive
Committee for Justice formed to help coordinate protests as Black students
in other communities organized similar demonstrations. In Houston, efforts

to integrate the lunch counters were led by Texas Southern University student Eldrewey Stearns, while Galveston's lunch counter sit-ins were led by sixteen-year-old Central High School student Kelton Sams.

HISTORIC SIDEBAR
CIVIL RIGHTS LEADERS: ELDREWEY STEARNS AND KELTON SAMS JR.

Eldrewey Joseph Stearns (1931–2020) was born and raised in Galveston. After he graduated from Central High School in 1949, he enlisted in the U.S. Army and enrolled in Michigan State University after he was discharged in 1953. With a bachelor's degree in political science and the intent to become a lawyer, Stearns moved to Houston in 1957 to study at the Thurgood Marshall School of Law at Texas Southern University. One night in 1959, Houston police stopped Stearns for having defective taillights. After police found a photograph of a White girl in his wallet, Stearns was arrested and beaten. In response to the injustice, Stearns encouraged thirteen fellow students at TSU to join him in lunch counter sit-ins. With the sit-ins held across the city on March 4, 1960, Stearns led a group of students to Weingarten's Super Market at 4110 Almeda Road for their first demonstration. The peaceful protest at Weingarten's would become known as the first successful sit-in in Texas.

Empowered by this success, Stearns led the students in other sit-ins that targeted lunch counters, movie theaters, restaurants and transit stations. During the protest movement, the Progressive Youth Association (PYA) formed, and Stearns was elected as the group's first president. Stearns and the TSU thirteen, as they came to be known, continued to protest across the city through 1964. The Houston chapter of the NAACP honored Stearns during the 1980s for his contributions to social and civil equality for minorities, and in 1984, Stearns was introduced to Dr. Thomas R. Cole, a professor at the Institute for the Medical Humanities at UTMB in Galveston.

Galveston native Eldrewey Stearns, recognized as one of the earliest civil rights leaders in Houston. *Courtesy of Old Central Cultural Center Inc.*

Over the next thirteen years, Cole and Stearns collaborated to write Stearns's autobiography, *No Color Is My Kind: The Life of Eldrewey Stearns and the Integration of Houston*, published in 1997. The city of Houston and TSU paid tribute to Stearns and the TSU thirteen in 2010 with the placement of a State of Texas Historic subject marker at the site of the old Weingarten's that documents the historic event. A scholarship in his name was also established at the University of Houston at Clear Lake by Congresswoman Sheila Jackson Lee.

As a sixteen-year-old student at Central High School, Galveston native Kelton Daniel Sams Jr. (1943–present) organized Galveston's department store lunch counter sit-ins in 1960. Inspired by the news of protests in Houston led by Eldrewey Stearns, Sams organized peaceful sit-ins at lunch counters across Galveston that began on March 11, 1960, at the W.F. Woolworth's on the corner of Market and 23rd Streets. Over the next two weeks, Sams organized more sit-ins while meetings were held between the all-White Galveston Ministerial Association, the all-Black Galveston Ministerial Alliance, local business owners and community leaders. As a result, on April 5, 1960, lunch counters were opened to everyone across the city of Galveston.

A new challenge arose in October 1960 after a Dairy Queen restaurant opened on the corner of Broadway and 26th Street. Sams led a group of students to the restaurant, where they ordered food from a window designated for Black patrons, after which the group entered the restaurant dining room and sat down to eat. When Sams and the students refused to leave at the management's request, they were arrested and charged with loitering. Margaret Armstrong stood in for her husband T.D. Armstrong, who was out of town, and paid their bail. A few weeks later, the charges were dropped and the dining room was opened to all patrons.

After Sams graduated from Central High School in 1961, he attended Texas Southern University and earned a bachelor's degree in economics in 1966. He remains a staunch civil rights advocate and is still involved in community and religious affairs. In recognition of his achievements, Sams was awarded the Excellence in Servant Leadership Award, presented

Kelton Sams organized Galveston's department store lunch counter sit-ins in 1961. *SC60_FF6, courtesy of the Rosenberg Library (Galveston, TX).*

in 2015 by UTMB, and an Image Award, presented by First Union Baptist Church. That same year, the NAACP named Sams an Unsung Hero Honoree, and the City of Galveston's mayor and city council issued a proclamation that declared January 29, 2015, Kelton D. Sams Day.

Sams's autobiography, an oral history titled *Growing up in Galveston Texas: Walls Came Tumbling Down*, recounts his life as a civil rights activist. Recorded in partnership with Texas Southern University in 2016, the recording is available online through the Portal to Texas History, a gateway of shared history administered by the University of North Texas in Denton.

5

CONTEMPORARY CELEBRATIONS
OF JUNETEENTH

The day was abundant in an era of want. Juneteenth planted firm roots within the racial caste system known as Jim Crow.…It was a time to reflect on Black progress, but also to remember that the limited version of freedom afforded to African Americans was not what had to be.
—Brandon Byrd, "The Living History of Juneteenth, Our Next National Holiday," GQ magazine, June 19, 2020

And, oh gosh, the food, it was wonderful. I remember they would have church service. All the women would wear white—and I don't know how they kept the wrinkles out of those beautiful white dresses. Men wore dark suits.
And I'd say they had a halleluiah time! We have come so far, and we still have much further to go.
—Tommie D. Boudreaux, retired Galveston ISD administrator, GHF Board of Directors, chair of African American Heritage Committee and Community Leader

As a child, all I knew up until I was an adult was segregation. So, Juneteenth was a lot of joy and fun for us. We went on hay rides on West Beach. We would roast hotdogs and marshmallows. So, it was a joyous occasion for us. Whereas the older adults had a solemn appearance about them—they were thankful and they were praying. There was a lot of food, food that now we call "soul food." But first they always prayed, had that gratitude to God, for seeing

them through. It's a happy yet sad remembrance. We commemorate and never forget from whence we come.
—*Mozellar Petteway, retired research associate, Hematology Department, University of Texas Medical Branch, Galveston; Old Central Cultural Center Inc. board of directors; and Galveston Community Leader*

My father rejuvenated it back in 1975, but before that time it was a big thing with the church back in the '50s and '40s, when I was a child, and that's when I started hearing about Juneteenth. My father put it on the front line again, and he hooked up with Al Edwards to bring it back to light, where it is now. It's important because it tells my future. It's my past that leads me to my future. It's an ongoing journey. My big dream is that it brings us together.
—*Lawrence Thomas, retired Galveston ISD teacher, coach and descendant of William Menard Thomas*

I remember Juneteenth celebrations when I was younger. We celebrated at the house where my dad always barbequed, my mom would cook the sides in the kitchen. Some other family members might come by. I always remember feeling happy and looking forward to that time of year. The tradition of cooking on Juneteenth was passed on from my grandmother here in Galveston to my mom.
—*Candice Lamb, NFL Sports journalist and social media coordinator, VSiN by DraftKings*

My activities have become learning activities.…Things have changed so that now I learn something different every year. And I pass something on every year. I think what we have now is the possibility of equality, if we all continue to strive for it. We need to be looking back as we continue to move forward, that's the importance of celebrating Juneteenth. I'm glad I lived to see what my ancestors only dreamed, and that's only possibly in this America.
—*Ella Lewis, retired Galveston ISD administrator and GHF African American Heritage Committee member*

The past is the past, we've got to recognize it and acknowledge it so we can go further.
—*Manuel Thomas, Galveston community leader and copastor at God's Kingdom and Restoration Ministries*

The understanding that the young ones had…was Juneteenth was about the watermelon, the red soda water.…It was like the picnic part of the celebration,

but actually the history of Juneteenth, the struggle,
that definitely needs to be taught.
—*Sheila Smith, manager, Wright-Cuney Recreation Center, City of Galveston*
Parks and Recreation

As African Americans from Galveston and other cities in Texas migrated to other areas of the country, they took Juneteenth with them. Today, June 19 is celebrated in more than two hundred cities throughout the United States. In Galveston and elsewhere, Juneteenth is observed with speeches and songs, picnics, parades and exhibits of Black history and art. In recent years, Galveston, the city where Juneteenth began, has centered its celebrations on a public reading of General Orders No. 3 at the Galveston County Courthouse. Following the courthouse ceremony, there is a procession to Reedy Chapel, where the Emancipation Proclamation is once again read as it was on that site on January 1, 1866.

As the memory and remembrance of emancipation passed into the twentieth century, Juneteenth became an established celebration, not just in Galveston but in many towns in Texas. For the most part, the celebrations took place in segregated cities or all-Black towns. Almost as if in reaction to these limits to equality, Juneteenth style became exuberant: extravagantly dressed floats and the finest of uniforms. Intricately decorated horse carriages were common in Galveston and in Houston.

While there was some recorded use of the name "Juneteenth" in the 1890s, by the early twentieth century, it was commonplace and seen in Galveston newspaper accounts of the day's celebrations. These accounts also provide glimpses of the Jim Crow attitudes of the day in the surprise expressed by reporters at the lack of violence, as noted in a *Galveston Daily News* report on Houston's celebration in June 1903:

QUIET CELEBRATION
Few Minor Offenses and Little Intoxication of Negros

The remarkable quietude of the three day's Juneteenth celebration in Houston is commented upon….Colored people from surrounding points have flocked in and enjoyed themselves. It has been a peaceable celebration with a few minor disturbances and little intoxication.

Also remarkable is the fact that these celebrations took place only three years after the city of Galveston was devastated by the great storm of 1900, after which Black Galvestonians played a huge role in the island's recovery and the rebuilding that followed.

EMANCIPATION DAY
Fortieth Anniversary of Freedom from Slavery Fittingly Celebrated by Colored People of Galveston

Yesterday marked the fortieth anniversary of the emancipation act in Texas, and the colored people of Galveston gave their annual celebration. The program of the day's events began at noon with a parade through the streets. The parade was headed by a brass band, and this was followed by several colored citizens and the anniversary committee in carriages. In the parade were a number of floats showing the advancement of the colored race since the first emancipation day.
—Galveston Daily News, *June 20, 1905*

Reference to the emancipation of the race will be made from the pulpits of several negro churches, it is announced. Texas is the only state, it is said, where the negroes observe June 19, the familiar Juneteenth, as emancipation day.
—Galveston Daily News, *June 19, 1921*

NEGROES HERE HAVE A QUIET HOLIDAY

All dressed up in the best frocks and suits, Galveston negroes yesterday celebrated Juneteenth, Emancipation Proclamation Day, in a gay if decorous manner. Watermelons were observed about the city and added to the pleasure of the day.
—Galveston Daily News, *June 20, 1928*

BARBECUE, RODEO FEATURE LOCAL JUNETEENTH PLANS

A huge four-hour-long rodeo and barbeque and numerous private parties and dances will feature the local negro population's observance of Juneteenth here. A 20-man band has been scheduled to play at the rodeo grounds. Barbeque and refreshments will be available to the estimated 3,000 negroes who are expected to attend the event.
—Galveston Daily News, *June 19, 1947*

NEGROES JOIN FOR JUNE 19 ANNUAL EVENT

A long weekend of fun, to be climaxed by a Juneteenth observance Monday, was under way in Galveston Sunday as thousands of negroes from throughout the state took part. Negro hotels and apartments at the beach front and downtown were packed. Singing and dancing programs were slated for Monday at taverns and cafes along the negro beach front.
—Galveston Daily News, *June 19, 1950*

The days of "monstrous and brilliant" parades in Galveston gave way to more private Juneteenth celebrations in the mid-twentieth century, with families gathering for beach parties and cookouts. Churches observed Emancipation Day with the reverent singing of the song "Lift Every Voice" (the official song of the National Association for the Advancement of Colored People) and the plea to remember the significance of June 19 and the joy of freedom. In the late 1940s, public observations of Juneteenth were held in Galveston at Wright Cuney Park. Both private and public celebrations continued to emphasize Black history, heroes and achievements. With the coming of integration and the civil rights movement in the 1950s and 1960s, the observance of Juneteenth diminished, with emphasis instead being directed toward the goal of interracial harmony and togetherness.

The 1970s saw a reemergence of public observance of the day, as African Americans became more aware of their cultural heritage, and on June 13, 1979, Texas governor William P. Clements Jr. signed into law a bill, sponsored by Representative Al Edwards (D, Houston), that made Juneteenth a state holiday, the first bill in the nation to do so. On June 19, 1979, Representative Edwards and city employee Doug Matthews, operating as the Galveston Juneteenth Committee, initiated a prayer vigil on the lawn of Ashton Villa. One year later, the first celebration of the state holiday for Juneteenth began at Ashton Villa in June 1980, with state representatives, local elected officials, Mr. Matthews and others present for the reading of the Emancipation Proclamation (and probably General Orders No. 3) and the annual prayer breakfast.

The 1980 event and the passage of the state legislation for a holiday was an affirmative act by Black Galvestonians to legitimize and create an inspirational experience based on the recognition of the first official state and local holiday for Juneteenth. To attract a crowd and inspire the community, the NAACP enhanced an undocumented account of June 19, 1865. The

Left: Former Texas state representative Albert Ely Edwards. *Courtesy of the "State Rep. Al Edwards Sr" Facebook page: https:// www.facebook.com/RepAlEdwardsSr/photos.*

Below: Representative Al Edwards (*center*) presides over Juneteenth celebrations at Ashton Villa in 1980. *Juneteenth Celebration Collection, SC_58_FF29_011, courtesy of the Rosenberg Library (Galveston, TX).*

1980 celebration of Juneteenth envisioned a recreation of General Gordon Granger's presence at Ashton Villa and the announcement of General Orders No. 3 from the balcony. This romanticized version of June 19, 1865, evoked a setting and a response from Galveston's enslaved community that may have occurred but is, to date, undocumented by historians (NAACP press release, May 29, 1980).

In 1981, the Texas Emancipation Day Commission was incorporated in Austin and San Antonio with Representative Edwards as a consultant (but not a member). Representative Edwards and the Galveston Juneteenth Committee erected a statue and commemorative marker at Ashton Villa in 2006 that is a smaller and less complex version than the one placed on the

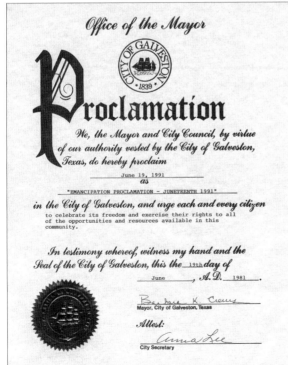

Above: A drill team marches down Ball Street during the 1991 Juneteenth parade. *Juneteenth Celebration Collection, SC_58_FF29_010, courtesy of the Rosenberg Library (Galveston, TX).*

Left: The City of Galveston's "Emancipation Proclamation: Juneteenth 1991." *Juneteenth Celebration Collection, MS91_0008_Box 1_FF3_1, courtesy of the Rosenberg Library (Galveston, TX).*

The Legislator, located on the lawn of Ashton Villa, honors State Representative Al Edwards and his successful efforts that established Juneteenth as a Texas holiday in 1980. *Courtesy of the Galveston Historical Foundation.*

Crowds gather for the Juneteenth ceremony on the porch of Ashton Villa in 2005. *Courtesy of the Galveston Historical Foundation.*

The Juneteenth celebration at Ashton Villa in 2012. *Courtesy of the Galveston Historical Foundation.*

state capitol grounds a decade later in 2016. For forty-two years, Ashton Villa has served as the site of a community Juneteenth celebration that recognizes the state holiday and was hosted by Representative Edwards until his death in 2020. The event is still titled the Al Edwards Annual Juneteenth Prayer Breakfast (modified to the Al Edwards Annual Juneteenth Celebration in 2020 during the COVID-19 pandemic).

Such contradictions between the essence of Juneteenth and the lived reality of most African Americans eventually came to a head in a new wave of the civil rights movement, in which the promise of Juneteenth became a demand for equal rights. This in turn reinvigorated the popularity of Juneteenth observations for the rest of the century and indeed into present times.

Juneteenth began its journey toward recognition throughout the country in 1979, when Representative Al Edwards succeeded in having the day declared a paid Texas State holiday. This is commemorated in the statue of *The Legislator* that now stands on the grounds of Ashton Villa, its pose evoking the very proclamation the holiday is meant to honor. Edwards's annual prayer breakfast and celebration, first held in 1979, continues to take place every Juneteenth at Ashton Villa.

In preparation for the celebration of the 150th anniversary of Juneteenth, a Texas State Historic subject marker dedicated to Juneteenth was erected by

The dedication of the State of Texas subject marker for Juneteenth in 2014. *Courtesy of the Galveston Historical Foundation.*

A Juneteenth subject marker, sponsored by GHF's African American Heritage Committee in 2014, is located at 22nd Street and the Strand, where the Osterman building once stood. *Courtesy of the Galveston Historical Foundation.*

On June 17, 2021, surrounded by dignitaries, President Joe Biden signed senate bill S.475 and enacted the Juneteenth National Independence Day Act. *Courtesy of the Executive Office of the President of the United States.*

the Galveston Historical Foundation and the Texas Historical Commission on the corner of the Strand and 22nd Street, where the Osterman building once stood. The marker signifies the importance of the location of Major General Granger's Union headquarters and subsequent issuance of General Orders No. 3.

During the COVID-19 pandemic, the annual Juneteenth celebration at Ashton Villa continued, with events livestreamed on social media. In 2021, on the 156th anniversary of the announcement of General Orders No. 3, President Joseph Biden signed into law the Juneteenth National Independence Day Act and created a national holiday that commemorates Juneteenth.

SUMMARY

Juneteenth is a not a new concept or story. Galvestonians and Texans have long understood the significance of the annual holiday. When "Juneteenth" moved forward as a national holiday rather than just a state and local holiday in 2021, the historical significance and newly realized meaning of the holiday spread across the United States and the world.

Galveston Historical Foundation's historical experience at Ashton Villa (1859) tells the local story of Juneteenth. It highlights, through images, historical text and personal stories, what Galveston Island was like in the 1860s and, to some degree, how it appears today. It may not be the complete Juneteenth story, but it is Galveston's Juneteenth story. Other communities in Texas and across the United States—and even in foreign countries—are telling their own stories and reconnecting to the formation of the holiday from the nineteenth century as it is appropriate and accurate.

Historians typically want to tell the story of our history with great precision and based on solid research. To that end, new information is still emerging from the extraordinary event on June 19, 1865, and revised interpretations are coming forward. Galveston Historical Foundation believes this project and the information provided to visitors and tourists is the most current interpretation on Juneteenth and provokes each person who experiences it to think a little deeper and broader about the national holiday.

This publication parallels the historical experience that is now centered at Ashton Villa and is an effort to share the research from the development of the experience, as well as the previously untold history of the Black community

The 1859 Ashton Villa, 2328 Broadway, the site of the annual Al Edwards Juneteenth celebrations since 1979. *Courtesy of the Galveston Historical Foundation.*

on Galveston Island. This work is fresh and new, as well as reflective of well-known history. It is, however, in the end, a sizeable accomplishment that makes our Galveston Juneteenth story personal for the many individuals who call the island home, even if they are now far away or gone.

ABOUT THE GALVESTON HISTORICAL FOUNDATION/AFRICAN AMERICAN HERITAGE COMMITTEE

Galveston Historical Foundation (GHF) was formed as the Galveston Historical Society in 1871 and merged with a new organization formed in 1954 as a nonprofit entity devoted to historic preservation and history in Galveston County. Over the last sixty years, GHF has expanded its mission to encompass community redevelopment, historic preservation advocacy, maritime preservation, coastal resiliency and the stewardship of historic properties. GHF embraces a broader vision of history and architecture that encompasses advancements in environmental and natural sciences and their intersection with historic buildings and coastal life and conceives of history as an engaging story of individual lives and experiences on Galveston Island from the nineteenth century to the present day.

GHF's African American Heritage Committee (AAHC) was formed in 2002 at Ashton Villa with over forty diverse citizens in attendance. The group elected Maggie Williams, a Galveston native and retired schoolteacher, as the first chairperson of the committee and adopted the mission statement to identify, commemorate and preserve historic sites important to African Americans and the Galveston community. Rosewood Cemetery was the first place of interest identified by the committee, and as members and other concerned citizens focused on clearing out the overgrown cemetery, others researched and documented the cemetery's history. Their efforts were rewarded in 2011 with a special public ceremony that unveiled a Texas Historical Commission (THC) Historic Texas Cemetery marker for Rosewood. Over the past twenty years, several chairpersons have presided

The current African American Heritage Committee. *From left to right*: Jami Durham (GHF staff), Tommie Boudreaux (chair), Diane Henderson, David O'Neal, Ella Lewis, Joan Hubert, Lillie Little and Alice Gastson. *Courtesy of the Galveston Historical Foundation.*

over the committee, and new members dedicated to the mission statement have joined the inaugural members who remain.

Current and past committee activities include GHF's annual Dickens on the Strand Victorian holiday festival, where it hosts a booth to raise funds for the ongoing maintenance of Rosewood, as well as the coordination of an annual essay contest in conjunction with Martin Luther King Day, summer Underground Railroad events for youth programs, Juneteenth choral performances at Ashton Villa and celebrations that surrounded the one hundred year anniversary of the Colored Branch of Galveston's Rosenberg Library, cosponsored by the Old Central Cultural Center. In 2014, the committee dedicated a Texas Historical Commission subject marker for Juneteenth, held in celebration with the 150th anniversary of U.S. general Gordon Granger's arrival in Galveston. The public ceremony and marker placement was hosted at 22nd Street and the Strand, where Granger's headquarters were once located. The committee also joined the Middle Passage Ceremonies and Port Markers Project in 2017 and dedicated a Middle Passage Marker on Galveston's historic harbor that honors the

forced migration of enslaved people. And on June 19, 2022, guided by the
AAHC, GHF opened the permanent interactive exhibit *And Still We Rise…
Galveston's Juneteenth Story*, located in the carriage house of the historic 1859
Ashton Villa. Published works by the committee and individual members
that document the island's Black history include *Galveston's African American
Historic Places & Pioneers* (2005), *African Americans of Galveston* (2013) and *Lost
Restaurants of Galveston's African American Community* (2021).

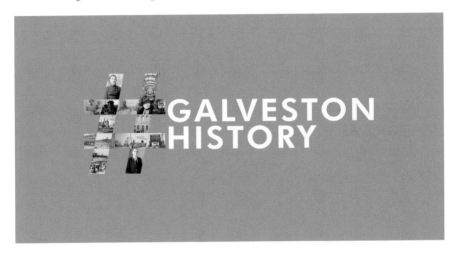

BIBLIOGRAPHY

"America's 100 Richest Negroes—Many Solid Gold Millionaires among Top Moneymakers in Business, Professions." *Ebony* 17, no. 7 (May 11, 1962): 130.

Austin American Statesman. "Holiday Is Official and Busy." June 9, 1980.

Austin Daily Texan. "New State Holiday Rotunda Ceremonies Kick Off Juneteenth." June 19, 1980.

Barrett, Anna P. *Juneteenth: Celebrating Freedom in Texas*. Fort Worth, TX: Eakin Press, 1999.

Beasley, Ellen. *The Alleys and Back Buildings of Galveston: An Architectural and Social History*. Houston, TX: Rice University Press, 1996.

Boudreaux, Tommie, and Alice Gatson. *African Americans of Galveston*. Charleston, SC: Arcadia Publishing, 2013.

Byrd, Brandon. "The Living History of Juneteenth, Our Next National Holiday." *GQ*, June 19, 2020. https://www.gq.com/story/the-living-history-of-juneteenth.

City Times (Galveston, TX). "Colored Citizens to Celebrate 19th of June." June 9, 1917.

———. "Cotton Jammers Park." June 20, 1914.

———. "Emancipation Day Celebrations." June 7, 1907.

———. "Emancipation Day Next Monday." June 17, 1916.

———. "Grand Free Barbecue Emancipation Day." June 11, 1904, supplement.

———. "Juneteenth in Galveston." June 20, 1914.

———. "19th of June a Big Celebration at Dickinson." May 27, 1916.

———. "Our Citizens Should Feel Proud." June 9, 1917.

———. "Some Progress in Fifty-One Years of Freedom." June 17, 1916.

———. "Take Notice." June 3, 1916.

Conner, Robert C. *General Gordon Granger: The Savior of Chickamauga and the Man Behind Juneteenth*. Havertown, PA: Casemate Publishers, 2013.

Cotham, Edward T. *Battle on the Bay: The Civil War Struggle for Galveston*. Austin: University of Texas Press, 1998.

———. *Juneteenth: The Story Behind the Celebration*. College Station: Texas A&M University Press, 2021.

Crouch, Barry A. *The Dance of Freedom: Texas African Americans During Reconstruction*. Austin: University of Texas Press, 2007.

Cuney-Hare, Maude. *Norris Wright Cuney: A Tribune of the Black People*. Austin: Steck-Vaugh Company, 1968.

Danky, James Phillip, and Maureen E. Hady. *African American Newspapers and Periodicals: A National Biography*. Boston, MA: Harvard University Press, 1998.

Davis, William C. *Three Roads to the Alamo: The Lives and Fortunes of David Crockett, James Bowie and William Barrett Travis*. New York: Harper Perennial. 1999.

Flake's Bulletin (Galveston, TX). "New Year's Day." January 2, 1866.

Fornell, Earl Wesley. *The Galveston Era: The Texas Crescent on the Eve of Secession*. Austin: University of Texas Press, 1961.

Galveston City Directory. Galveston, TX: Galveston News, publisher, 1859–67, 1870, 1872.

Galveston City Directory. Galveston, TX: Shaw and Blaylock, publishers, 1868–69.

Galveston City Directory. Galveston, TX: John H. Heller, publisher, 1874, 1876–77, 1878–79, 1880–81.

Galveston City Directory. Galveston, TX: Fayman and Reilly's, publisher, 1875–76.

Galveston City Directory. Galveston, TX: Charles D. Morrison and Joseph V. Fourmy, publishers, 1881–1957.

Galveston City Directory. Galveston, TX: R.L. Polk and Co., publishers, 1958–96.

Galveston County Daily News. "2022 Juneteenth Weekend Continues." June 18, 2022.

Galveston Daily News. "City Names First Negro Firemen." November 22, 1957.

———. "Four Stores Are Involved, No Violence." March 12, 1960.

———. "Integration Quiet Here, No Incidents as Stores Open Counters to All." April 6, 1960.

———. "Island Negro Education Dies, John R. Gibson Was Also Diplomat." December 13, 1948.

———. "Juneteenth Celebration Set Today." June 19, 1980, 2.

———. "Juneteenth Was Celebrated Thursday." June 20, 1980.

———. "Negroes to Be Named to Fire Department." November 3, 1957.

———. "Negro 'Sitdowner' Activity Spreads." March 13, 1960.

———. "Negro 'Sitdowns' Close Counters." March 12, 1960.

———. "Negro Teacher Group to Cease, Join TSTA." August 17, 1966.

———. "State Capital Notes: Chartered the Nineteenth of June Emancipation Celebration and Historical Association of Galveston." September 5, 1886.

———. "State Representative Al Edwards from Houston Addresses Gathering at Ashton Villa." June 21, 1980.

Galveston News. "Bastrop Emancipation—Jones Speaks." June 20, 1878.

———. "Board Has Power to Separate Races." June 14, 1922.

———. "Emancipation Celebration." June 20, 1872.

———. "Emancipation Celebration." June 13, 1886.

———. "Emancipation Day." June 20, 1874.

———. "Emancipation Day." June 20, 1878.

———. "Emancipation Day at Brenham." June 20, 1878.

———. "Liberty—The Colored People Celebrate." June 20, 1878.

———. "Lions Club Calls on City to Exclude Negroes from the Boulevard." June 5, 1922.

———. "Marlin—The Emancipation Celebration." June 20, 1878.

———. "Officials Again Postpone Beach Segregation Following Heated Argument." July 18, 1922.

————. "Petition Seeks Removal of Negroes from Beach." June 16, 1922.

————. "Procession Yesterday." June 21, 1870, 3.

————. "The Provost Marshal General." June 20, 1865.

Gordon-Reed, Annette. *On Juneteenth*. Washington, D.C.: National Geographic Books, 2021.

Green, Victor Hugo. *The Negro Motorist Green-Book*. New York: Victor Hugo Green, publisher, 1936–66.

Hafertepe, Kenneth. *A History of Ashton Villa*. Austin: Texas State Historical Association, 1991.

Hales, Douglas. *A Southern Family in White and Black: The Cuneys of Texas*. College Station: Texas A&M University Press, 2003.

Handbook of Texas Online. "Juneteenth." www.tsha.utexas.edu/handbook/online/juneteenth.

McComb, David G. *Galveston: A History*. Austin: University of Texas Press, 1986.

Moreland, Kenneth. *Special Report: Lunch Counter Desegregation in Corpus Christi, Galveston and San Antonio, Texas*. Atlanta, GA: Southern Regional Council, May 10, 1960.

Pelz, Matthew. Interview with Lucious Pope. May 5, 2017. Recording and partial transcript available at Preservation Resource Center, Galveston Historical Foundation (Galveston, TX).

Press Release and Statement: Emancipation Day. From the office of Al Edwards, state representative District 146. June 13, 1979.

Press Release and Statement: Juneteeth. From the office of the National Association for the Advancement of Colored People (Galveston, TX). May 29, 1980.

Press Release: 66th Legislature, Regular Session, Emancipation Day in Texas. Holidays, chapter 481, H.B. no. 1016. From the office of Al Edwards, state representative District 85. June 13, 1979.

Ravage, John W. *Black Pioneers, Images of the Black Experience on the North American Frontier*. Salt Lake City: University of Utah Press, 2008.

Rawick, George P., ed. *The American Slave: A Composite Autobiography Supplement*. Series 2, Texas Narratives. Vol. 9, no. 8. Westport, CT: Greenwood Press, 1979.

Sance, Melvin M. *The Afro-American Texans*. San Antonio: University of Texas, Institute of Texan Cultures, 1987.

The Slave Narratives of Texas. Austin: State House Press, 1997.

Stephen F. Austin State University, East Texas Digital Archives. "Texas Runaway Slave Project." https://digital.sfasu.edu/digital/collection/RSP.

Texas Folklore Society. *Juneteenth Texas: Essays in African-American Folklore.* Denton, TX; University of North Texas Press, 1996.

Texas Lifestyle Magazine. "Living Texas, Celebrating Juneteenth and General Orders No. 3." June 16, 2020.

ABOUT THE CONTRIBUTORS

Tommie Dell Boudreaux, born on the island, is a retired Galveston independent school administrator who graduated from the historic Central High School. She serves on the Galveston Historical Foundation's board of directors and is the current chair of the foundation's African American Heritage Committee. She is a member of the Old Central Cultural Center board of directors and Golden Life member of Galveston's Delta Sigma Theta Sorority, Incorporated, where she is the chapter historian and chairperson of the sorority's heritage and archives. She also serves as president of the Galveston School Employees Federal Credit Union. Her previous published works include the books *African Americans of Galveston* and *Lost Restaurants of Galveston's African American Community*, as well as multiple local newspaper articles, "Ninth Annual Coats and Book Drive Underway," "Join in on the Spirit of King's Dream," "Red and White Luncheon to Honor Couples," "Enjoy Some Good Food" and "Come Honor Houston's Hero."

Alice M. Gatson is a retired biomedical technologist. Born on the island, she graduated from the historic Central High School and HBCU Huston-Tillotson University. She is an active member of Galveston's

Alpha Kappa Alpha sorority chapter and the Old Central Cultural Center, and she has served as chair of Galveston Historical Foundation's African American Heritage Committee. Her published works include *African Americans of Galveston*, coauthored with Tommie Boudreaux; *Lost Restaurants of Galveston's African American Community*; and medical articles, including "Evaluation of Mycobacteria Growth Indicator Tubes for Susceptibility Testing of Mycobacterium Tuberculosis to Isoniazid and Rifampin-Diagnostic Microbiology and Infectious Disease."

Jami Durham is a longtime employee of the Galveston Historical Foundation (GHF) with experience in museum management, event planning, specialized research and writing. Employed by GHF since 1998, her professional duties include the management of GHF's Preservation Resource Center and the administration of GHF Preservation Services programs that include the 1900 Storm Survivor Plaque and Texas Gulf Coast Windstorm Exemptions. She works closely with the GHF's African American Heritage Committee and assisted with its publications *African Americans of Galveston* and *Lost Restaurants of Galveston's African American Community*. In 2013, she coauthored *Galveston: Playground of the Southwest* with W. Dwayne Jones. She is a current member of the Galveston County Historical Commission, a graduate of Leadership Galveston (class of 2000) and a past Landmark Commissioner for the City of Galveston.

W. Dwayne Jones began as the executive director of GHF in December 2006. He is a graduate of Trinity University in San Antonio, with a bachelor of arts degree in history and Asian studies, and holds a master's degree in urban and regional planning from George Washington University in Washington, D.C. In 2020, he completed the requirements for a PhD from UTMB in medical humanities (the history of medicine). Dr. Jones served as the executive director of Preservation Dallas from 2000 to 2006 and, prior to that, worked with the National Register of Historic Places programs at the Texas Historical Commission. He has published works and lectured on historic roadside architecture, including a guidebook to historic gas stations in Texas with TxDOT. Dwayne is a former chairman of the National Alliance of Preservation Commissions and the president of Preservation Texas. He is currently the vice-president of the American Easement Foundation and also serves on the board of Build Galveston.

Visit us at
www.historypress.com